Considerations for Culturally Informed Leadership

Contemporary Perspectives on Leadership Learning

Series Editor
Kathy L. Guthrie

This series is dedicated to contemporary perspectives on leadership learning, which includes leadership teaching, education, development, and scholarship. It is intended to appeal to academic researchers, leadership scholars, leadership educators, and university instructors looking for thought-provoking reference material for classroom use. The purpose of the series is to highlight foundational knowledge and emerging innovations in scholarship on curriculum, pedagogy, and methodology of teaching and learning in leadership. Each book showcases a different topic critical to the research and practice of leadership teaching and learning. With this approach, the mission of the series is to examine the complexities of leadership learning from a variety of perspectives to give the audience access to breadth and depth of scholarship in this area, as well as provide contemporary reference material and textbooks for leadership learning in the classroom.

OTHER TITLES IN THE SERIES

Considerations for Culturally Informed Leadership

Moving Toward the Future

Kathy L. Guthrie

Florida State University, USA

And

Darren E. Pierre

University of Maryland-College Park, USA

emerald
PUBLISHING

United Kingdom – North America – Japan
India – Malaysia – China

Emerald Publishing Limited
Emerald Publishing, Floor 5, Northspring, 21-23 Wellington Street, Leeds LS1 4DL

First edition 2026

Copyright © 2026 by Emerald Publishing Limited.
All rights of reproduction in any form reserved.

Cover design: Carla Harvey/TNQ

Reprints and permissions service
Contact: www.copyright.com

British Library Cataloguing in Publication Data
A catalogue record for this book is available from the British Library

ISBN: 978-1-80592-470-8 (Print hardback)
ISBN: 978-1-80592-472-2 (Print paperback)
ISBN: 978-1-80592-469-2/978-1-80592-471-5 (Ebook)

Typeset by TNQ Tech
Cover design by TNQ Tech

CONTENTS

CHAPTER 1

SITUATING SELF IN CULTURALLY INFORMED LEADERSHIP LEARNING

The world is a big place. The United Nations (2022) estimated that by 2058 there will be approximately 10 billion people in the world. 10 billion people. Wow, just that number is hard to conceptualize. When you think about those billions of people, there are countless diverse ways of living, communities, and cultures. The diversity of our world continues to expand with multi-ethnicities, ways to worship, abilities, lived experiences, and so on. With the diversity of the world's population, not only learning about different cultures and ways of being are important, but so is understanding how to engage in leadership, connect with others, and create positive change. The focus of this book is the explore the process of leadership in various cultural contexts, a global context. More specifically, the focus of this book is YOU. Not the authors, but YOU and how you are situated in the multi-faceted, multicultural world around you. We are situating this book with self by exploring how to understand ourselves (Chapter 2), how we learn and more specifically learn leadership (Chapter 3), how we engage in diverse cultures around the world (Chapter 4) and how we connect culture and ideas to the leadership process as both a leader and a follower (Chapter 5). Below you see the progression of culturally informed leadership learning (Figure 1.1), which is the journey you are about to embark on.

It is important to note we believe that anyone can be a leader and that you do not need a title or hold a specific position. We also believe leadership is a process that includes leaders and followers engaging together in

Considerations for Culturally Informed Leadership, pages 1–11
Copyright © 2026 by Emerald Publishing Limited
doi:10.1108/978-1-80592-469-220251001

Figure 1.1 Progression of culturally informed leadership learning.

a specific context (more on that later). With those things in mind, we are excited to engage on this journey of leadership learning and self-exploration with you.

PURPOSE OF THIS BOOK

We hope you picked up this book because you are interested in leadership and how the process of leadership can and should be considered in global contexts. We hope you are excited to reflect on yourself and how you engage in various cultures, as well as excited to learn more about leadership and moving your leadership learning journey forward. This book is about just that. As mentioned above, we situate the entire book in self, meaning each person reading this book has the opportunity to reflect on themself and deeply think about themselves as a learner, engager, and connecter in various cultural contexts. This book is relatively short and hopefully you will observe how the material is shared in multiple ways and asks you to pause and think about yourself, leadership, and engaging in global contexts in new ways.

What signifies the difference between "leadership" and "global leadership" is the emphasis on the need to be responsive to cultural differences and relationship complexities (Mendenhall et al., 2018). We understand and acknowledge the term global leadership has often been the traditional language around leading in various cultural contexts. However, after much reflection and conversations with colleagues and friends around the world, we decided that global leadership might not be the best terminology for what we want this book to be. For some that term may mean that you strive to lead the world in a specific area, which may be true for some, but not what we are intending for this book. We also debated about intercultural leadership but felt that was not quite right because it may represent various cultures within a Western context, as the word intercultural is so often used in the United States. We also considered culturally influenced but felt the word influence signaled a passive verb then active. However, those conversations led us to culturally informed leadership, which nailed what this book is about. Learning, engaging, and connecting with and in various cultural contexts are critical to **culturally informed leadership**. Culture refers to customs and social beliefs that create the norms of a specific nation, people, or larger social group. Informing yourself about various cultures other than yours, perhaps by watching the news, immersing yourself with others from a culture different than yours, learning about the history and significant traditions of a culture are all aspects of informing yourself about contexts.

Hopefully, after reading this book you will not only reflect on your thoughts, behaviors, and engagement with others more deeply, but also lean into exploring how your leadership learning journey can drastically develop in different cultural contexts by informing yourself. The first chapter will discuss the definition of leadership as well as provide tips on how to fully use this book. Chapter 2 will explore the process of better understanding self. The third chapter will discuss how we are all learners and more specifically how we need to situate ourselves in various cultural contexts as learners and how that influences our leadership learning journeys. Chapter 4 will explore how we can and need to focus on engaging in cultural contexts to enhance our leadership development. Chapter 5 will focus on how being a connecter of ideas, people, and context is critical to leadership learning. Finally, in the last chapter, we will bring it all together.

WHAT IS LEADERSHIP?

Let's first discuss leadership as a broad concept. You see the word leadership everywhere. Think about all the places you see the word leadership and how people talk about it. Even doing a quick Google search of the word "leadership" you will see it being used as a noun, verb, and adjective. Over four billion results come up when you do a search for the "definition of leadership." This can be overwhelming-four billion (eek)! To make sure we are all on the same page about this complex concept of leadership, we want to dig more into what leadership means.

Leader and leadership are often confused and misused. Guthrie and Jenkins (2018) stated it clearly, "Confusion frequently results in carelessly interchanging the language of the person (leader) and the process (leadership). When used interchangeably, leadership becomes the work of one versus all" (p. 5). We believe that **leadership** is **socially constructed**, which means this multifaceted phenomenon is defined and practiced differently depending on one's lived experiences (Billsberry, 2009; Guthrie et al., 2021). We believe it is important to clarify the language of leadership so that learning about and practicing it can be easier.

Another way to think about the process of leadership is in a visual of a triangle (Guthrie & Devies, 2024). In this triangle (see Figure 1.2), the process of leadership is at the center. Leader, follower, and context are located at each of the points around the triangle.

To engage in the process of leadership, you need the three aspects of leader, follower, and context. Context can be the situation, setting, or environment in which leadership unfolds. The origin of the word context is Latin meaning "weaving together" (Harper, 2024). Think of context as the

Context

Leadership

Follower   Leader

Figure 1.2   Leadership triangle. Reprinted with permission from Devies, B., and Guthrie, K. L. Copyright 2023.

physical space, the actions of everyone involved, including the complexities and nuances of how others engage with each other and the physical space. In other words, it is being able to see the big picture of what is going on. Although most leadership theories do not take context into account during the leadership process, we are centering this book on how to lead in various cultural contexts. We cannot overstate the importance of context here. Think of it this way: how you lead in your student organization or with friends likely looks different than how you lead at work which probably looks different than how you lead in your family. You are still the same person, but how you lead and follow likely shifts depending on the context. It is important to be congruent with your personal values, but also adaptable depending on the situation you are in. This is especially true for the various cultural contexts you may encounter.

Implicit leadership theory (Lord & Maher, 1991) is another concept important to keep in mind when exploring leadership, especially in various cultural contexts. This theory suggests people have preconceived ideas and mental models about what is considered effective leadership. However, this definition of effectiveness varies depending on the person. This is like the idea of social construction that we previously mentioned because these mental models are formed through personal experiences and influences of the culture one grows up in. Implicit leadership theories especially vary greatly across different cultures.

BELIEFS ABOUT LEADERSHIP IN VARIOUS CULTURAL CONTEXTS

Now that you understand that leadership is a process that includes leader, follower, and context, we want to share some additional foundational beliefs regarding the leadership process in various cultural contexts. You may or may not agree with all these points, but it is important to know where we are coming from as authors. These beliefs include:

- **Anyone Can be a Leader.** Yes, anyone can engage in the process of leadership as a leader. Our first exposure to leaders is to those in positions of power, whether that is a parent, older sibling, teacher, or coach. However, leaders do not need to have a formal position of authority to work with others to collectively reach a goal. That can be anyone from any cultural context!
- **Leadership is Learned.** An outdated belief about leadership is that leaders are born, not made. This was a historic understanding of leadership, when people thought that the characteristics a person held determined if they were a leader or not. However, most skills and competencies needed for leadership can be learned. When focusing on leading in various cultural contexts, leadership is not what only needs to be learned, but also learning about different cultures. Recognizing cultural differences and learning to navigate various countries with diverse cultures within them is important. We will discuss more about being a learner in Chapter 3.
- **Being Open to Discomfort.** Striving to develop as a leader in various cultural contexts requires being open to learn, listen, and understand others' perspectives (Nirenberg, 2002). Discomfort will certainly arise as you interact with people from different cultures and have new experiences. It is important to remember that a global mindset does not come naturally for most (Nirenberg, 2002) because it is constantly challenging your way of knowing and being with new ways.
- **Leadership is Relational.** Relationships are important. Period. In the process of leadership, especially in various cultural contexts, relationships are important. Leaders and followers need to foster and cultivate genuine, authentic, and meaningful relationships when navigating cultural contexts. Some cultures lead from a collective framework and place community ideals at the heart of their leadership engagement. Focusing genuine relationships can lead to effective change while honoring community ideals in many cultural contexts.
- **Best Leaders are Also Followers.** As discussed, the process of leadership requires both leaders and followers in a specific context. The interactions of leaders and followers occur between them and are fluid in nature. In some contexts, you may be serving as a leader one minute and the next as a follower. The best leaders know when to follow and when to lead.
- **Effective Leadership Requires Management Skills.** Leadership and management are two concepts intricately connected. Oftentimes

leadership and management are discussed as opposite concepts; however, they are connected. Mastery of both sets of skills and understanding when to use what is essential in becoming a great leader and follower. When being a culturally informed leader, connecting how to use both leadership and management skills in various cultural contexts are essential for success.

LEADING IN VARIOUS CULTURAL CONTEXTS

This book focuses on learning leadership in various cultural contexts. As we mentioned, it is focused on self, that means you. There are several concepts, skills, and values that enhance one's leadership identity, capacity, and efficacy, especially in various cultural contexts. To learn, engage, and be a change agent in the world, we need to explore these different skills and how we can work to enhance our own knowledge and practice of them. When we practice leadership, we are building our identity as global leader, enhancing our capacity with skill development, and increasing our efficacy to lead in various cultural contexts.

We visualize the concepts, skills, and values we are discussing as a puzzle. As you see in the visual below (Figure 1.3), this global puzzle is something

Figure 1.3 Culturally informed puzzle.

that takes time to understand and put together. In fact, it is a puzzle that you will continue to work on for your entire life. This puzzle is your leadership learning journey.

LEADERSHIP IDENTITY, CAPACITY, AND EFFICACY DEVELOPMENT

Since this book is based in YOUR development as a learner, engager, and connector, focusing on leadership identity, capacity, and efficacy development is critical. Identity, capacity, and efficacy are pathways to learning leadership. As you can see in the figure below, identity, capacity, and efficacy are the pathways to learning leadership. Active exchange between the individual and the leadership process is essential to leadership development (see Figure 1.4). These three aspects of leadership development are interconnected, as you will see throughout this book.

Just like leadership, identity is socially constructed (Jones & Abes, 2013). Your identity is constantly evolving and has multiple dimensions at any time. When looking at your whole self, exploring these multiple dimensions are best appreciated when looking at it in relation to each other. More on this later. Another important aspect of leadership learning is capacity. This is the knowledge, skills, and talents that contribute to the overall ability to engage in leadership (Dugan, 2017). Efficacy is believing in your overall ability to be successful in leadership (Beatty & Guthrie, 2021). We will touch on identity, capacity, and efficacy throughout this book to support your leadership learning in various cultural contexts.

USING THIS BOOK

This book may have words that you are unsure what they mean. If you see a bolded word (which you should have already seen a few), these are key terms we think are important for your leadership learning journey.

Figure 1.4 Pathways to leadership learning. Adapted from Beatty & Guthrie (2021).

Some may have formal definitions we share, and some may need more exploration. We think these terms are a good start in building a strong foundation of engaging in culturally informed leadership. Also, there are images throughout the book that will encourage you to pause and reflect on content, and hopefully engage you in ways that will enhance your leadership learning. Although most of these questions and activities are at the end of each chapter, there will be moments of pause throughout each chapter as well. Brief descriptions of these ways for you to engage with the content are below, as well as questions and activities for you to start.

In this chapter, we have discussed the puzzle pieces of leadership, leader, follower, and context. In Chapter 2, we discuss understanding self through experiencing cultural shock (Ferraro & Broidy, 2017), emotionally intelligent leadership (Shankman et al., 2015), and interrelated aspects of culture (Ferro, 2009). Throughout several chapters, we will discuss the culturally relevant leadership learning model (Bertrand Jones et al., 2016) specifically leadership identity, capacity, and efficacy development. Self as a learner is the focus of Chapter 3 in which topics include unconscious bias (Stanford, 2022) and the leadership learning framework (Guthrie & Jenkins, 2018). In Chapter 4, we discuss self as an engager where cultural competencies will be highlighted. Contributing to positive change is discussed in Chapter 5. Finally in Chapter 6, we discuss how being a culturally informed leader is about thriving and being in a constant state of growth.

Chapter Framing. In each remaining chapter, you will see this image of a picture frame. This icon will be seen at the beginning of the chapter, as it will be used to frame the content of the chapter. This will help you engage in the learning by giving you thoughts and perhaps offer questions to consider as you work your way through the material.

Stop! Think About It! This image of a stop sign is to alert you to critical moments throughout the chapter. These moments are for you to pause and think about the information we are providing. At these points we might ask you to reflect on the content meaning or ask you to apply what we are discussing to your own experiences.

REFLECT ON YOUR OWN

You will be provided questions in this section to reflect on the chapter content. Take some time, by yourself, to consider these questions and how you can apply the concepts discussed in your own life.

- How do you define leadership? Write a two to three sentence definition of leadership. How do you define culturally informed leadership? How do your own experiences and observations of various cultural contexts shape your understanding of leadership?
- As discussed, leadership is a process with a leader and follower within a context. How does the context in which leadership occurs influence how you define it? Or does it? What about more specifically a cultural context?
- What role do followers play in defining effective leadership? What do they do or what characteristics do they have that make them a critical part of the process of leadership? How do you see this playing out when the leader and follower are from different cultural contexts?

REFLECT WITH A FRIEND

With a friend, classmate, or family member, continue your reflection with the questions provided in this section. These questions can serve as guide to dialogue with others, which is a good way to make meaning of your leadership learning.

- Knowing how to be a good follower is important for a person to be a good leader. How do you know when you should be a follower? As a follower, how can you best support a leader? How does learning, engaging, and connecting as a culturally informed leader contribute (or not) to this?
- How do think cultural differences influence one's definition of leadership, styles of leading, and approaches followership in various regions around the world?
- How does internationalization influence the role and responsibilities of leaders and followers in today's interconnected world?

LEVELING UP!

Leveling up in your leadership learning involves engaging in activities to enhance your knowledge development by reflecting and practicing skills. Two activities will be provided at the end of each chapter to support your continued leadership learning journey.

Activity 1: Your Leadership Definition

Considering leadership is socially constructed, it is important to think about how you define leadership. This book is about being culturally informed; however, thinking about how you define leadership broadly is important before focusing on how it is culturally informed. Answer the following questions to help guide your own development of a leadership definition for you to operate from. Please write in the book, in a notebook, on your computer or phone.

What are 3-4 main points of leadership that come to your mind? Jot down the words or phrase here.

Who are leaders you have most admired in your life? What made you admire them? Is it specific skills or abilities they have?

Recall moments when you were especially proud of how you engaged in leadership. What did you do? How did others respond to you in the process?

From your answers to the above questions, construct a 2-3 sentence definition of leadership. Your thoughts from the questions bring forward aspects of leadership that are important to you. While this 2-3 sentence definition will not be perfect, it is a place to start. Please know that this definition should evolve as you develop as a person.

Activity 2: Drawing on Your Culturally Informed Leadership Experience

Each of us engage in the leadership daily, whether that is as a leader and/or as a follower. The leadership triangle (Guthrie & Devies, 2024) was introduced in this chapter to visually share how the leadership process is made up of leaders, followers, and context. Think about a time you have observed leadership in the last week that was in a different cultural context. This can be something observed on the news, in a public space, or on your campus. Use the space below to sketch the leadership experience you are thinking about. In your picture, label what is context, who the followers are, and who the leaders are.

Draw your leadership experience below:

Now, once you have drawn your leadership experience in which you are thinking about, reflect on these questions:

1. Why did you choose the experience you did to draw? What makes it important to you?
2. Have you ever thought about a leadership experience in the frames of context, follower, and leader?
3. How did a different culture show up in your observation?
4. What is one element you drew and labeled that may have surprised you?

CHAPTER 2

UNDERSTANDING SELF IN VARIOUS CULTURAL CONTEXTS

When you get on an airplane, one of the first instructions given is to put your oxygen mask on first before helping others; in leadership, that same approach is taken. Like an oxygen mask on a plane, leadership starts with self. In this chapter, we explore leadership in relationship to self-awareness, and its importance, especially in the context of leading in multi-national/cultural settings.

Leadership starts with oneself is not a new concept (HERI, 1996), but in the realm of global leadership, it takes on a greater level of importance. Who are you? This is a central question to leadership. To take the question a step further, its ascertaining what are your core beliefs, interest, and values. As a person committed to global leadership, self-awareness and the act of self-questioning is necessary to facilitate a productive acclimation to a new environment in your intent to successfully work, lead, and serve amongst international groups and teams. Like leadership, the work of self-awareness is an ongoing, lifelong process. The question of "who are you?" cannot be answered in one day, but rather is answered in context.

In this chapter, we explore the importance of self-awareness in connection to emotional intelligence. The chapter includes a discussion on leadership identity, capacity, and efficacy and how all three work in connection with one another to support your success in acclimating to a new region of the world. The concept of culture shock is explored and

Considerations for Culturally Informed Leadership, pages 13–24
Copyright © 2026 by Emerald Publishing Limited
All rights of reproduction in any form reserved.
doi:10.1108/978-1-80592-469-220251003

explained as a natural response to encountering a set of customs, traditions, and beliefs that differ from yours. Finally, the chapter concludes with personal reflection prompts for you to consider as you continue to broaden your global leadership competencies. Throughout the chapter, examples are made that refer to working on studying abroad, but in the broader sense, what this chapter aims to do is support you in being a culturally informed leader.

UNDERSTANDING SELF IN CONTEXT OF CULTURALLY INFORMED LEADERSHIP

Self-awareness can be defined as a person's capacity to identify, and comprehend their emotions, feelings and beliefs, what drives those, and their impact as it relates to connecting with others (Northouse, 2022). Think back to those monumental experiences in your life; for some, it was going to college, others it was starting a new job, for many it was the loss of a loved one—and for others it was all three. Those "crucible moments" that shape your core values, considerations, and thoughts are what factor into the composition of who you are. Having a core understanding of yourself, asking those key reflective questions: What do I value? What were those monumental experiences of life? How did they shape me? The answers to those questions will help in the preparatory work required to work, study, or live abroad.

The time is now to examine these questions. To wait to interrogate who you are until you are exposed to culturally differences or even until you go abroad to visit, or study is fraught with challenges. For many the experience of being in a foreign land will test many values and have someone question core assumptions regarding their identity (Ferraro & Broidy, 2017). Our recommendation is you take time to do the reflection of who you are so that you can be clear about your values, assumptions and needs while being abroad.

For example, if you know that family is a core value for you, and you have made plans to study abroad in a country 5,000 miles away from home, have you considered what you will need to do to remain connected to family in the event you become homesick? If you are someone who needs time alone to recharge, how will you ensure time for solitude when in a study abroad program where much of your time is spent in groups? If you are someone who values the "creature comforts" of home, what will you do to make sure you have some of those novelties of home with you while you are abroad? As a culturally informed leader, committed to global learning, the work on yourself and awareness of your core values are imperative to find success navigating a different region of the world.

EMOTIONAL INTELLIGENT LEADERSHIP

Emotional intelligent leadership is a leadership theory grounded in self-awareness). Theorists state that emotionally intelligent leaders should be conscious of self, conscious of others, and consciousness of context (Shankman et al., 2015). Emotional intelligence (EQ) is important to the culturally informed leadership. Emotional intelligence is supported by three pillars: consciousness of self, consciousness of others, and consciousness of context. In other words, how we relate to ourselves, how we relate to others, and how we relate to our context fosters or dismantles connections between groups, teams, and organizations. Let's explore the three pillars of emotional intelligence. As you consider each pillar, think about how easy (or difficult) EQ is for you to practice. Like with many things, the more we work at EQ, the more proficient we become in engaging it in practice. What follows is a deeper explanation of each of the three pillars of emotional intelligent leadership.

Consciousness of Self

This first pillar of emotional intelligence centers on self-awareness. The culturally informed leader needs to be aware of who they are, their values, and how their lived experiences and environment have shaped their cultural considerations. Self-awareness has us understand our strengths and limitations and communicate those powerfully to others. As a person committed to leading in a global context, your ability to commit to mastering consciousness of self is imperative to your success in navigating a new region and building community with others to move forward shared goals and initiatives.

Consciousness of Others

The notion of being aware of the thoughts, feelings, and perspectives of others is not an easy task; it requires unbridling preconceived judgments and considerations of what are the operating norms. For example, you may visit a region of the world and upon observation, you may say to yourself, "wow, everyone speaks so softly" or "how come everyone walks so slow?" Neither of these observations are based in fact, but rather they are based on judgments grounded in previous experiences. One of the key distinctions in global leadership and its domestic counterpart is looking at those judgments, honoring them, and reevaluating observations in the objective versus the subjective. The observation moves from "wow, everyone speaks so softly" to "people are speaking" (Osland, 2012). Shifting perspective and letting go of judgment makes for greater opportunities for connection and strengthening relationships with others.

The observation examples shared were comparatively low stakes, but there will be times when you may find yourself in a space where what you are observing is in strong opposition to your core beliefs. Perspectives on human rights, social justice, and personal liberties are described differently worldwide. Like with the examples shared earlier, your ability to forego judgments is important in sustaining and building connections. This is not to say you should divorce yourself from your values, but rather, you should take those values in consideration of the context you are asked to serve and lead.

Consciousness of Context

So, you have done the work to discover the core aspects of you, and how who you are is impacted by others and the environment. Furthermore, you have explored understanding others, withholding judgments, and making concerted efforts to allow the cultural influences of the region you are exploring to support you in developing strong relationships with colleagues and peers. Now is the opportunity to look at context, the third pillar of emotional intelligent leadership (Shankman et al., 2015). As a leader, your ability to analyze, observe, and make determinations for how to engage is critical to navigating unfamiliar cultural spaces.

One of the ways context plays out in culturally informed leadership is through communication styles and patterns. People from various regions speak in different ways. Even when the same language is spoken, the ways that communication takes place can vary from region to region. Korac-Kakabadse et al. (2001) discuss the notion of low-context and high-context countries. Low-context cultural communities speak in direct ways, where expectations are clearly defined and the need for interpretation is minimal. In contrast, high-context cultures rely on expression and nonverbal modalities of communication (voice inflection, gestures, etc.) to fully convey thoughts, feelings, and emotions. Communication patterns matter, understanding the cultural context in how others communicate will benefit you in developing your skillset as a culturally informed leader.

> **STOP**
>
> Consider how you have seen emotional intelligence in action. Where have you seen in yourself or in others the practice of consciousness of self, others, and context? Where have you seen EIL practice well? Where have you seen it practiced poorly?

CULTURAL CONSIDERATIONS

Beyond groups and teams, a leader needs to consider the environmental context in which they are leading. Our world is full of dynamic political, ceremonial, and environmental occurrences that all require our attention when thinking of how we lead. Ferraro (2009) offers interrelated considerations when looking at various aspects of culture: government, education, religion, marriage, family, medicine, technology, and art. These interrelated aspects of culture can inform the context for how you will work and lead in a foreign cultural setting.

In today's global society, someone can look at any of the aspects of culture listed by Ferraro (2009) and see how they inform the ways people in a society move, express themselves and interact with one another. Table 2.1 offers examples of questions to consider when looking at each of the various aspects of culture as Ferraro (2009) outlines.

Each of the considerations posed for the various interrelated aspects of culture can support you in learning and responding effectively to the context of the region.

IDENTITY AND EFFICACY IN CULTURALLY INFORMED LEADERSHIP

We did a dive into communication patterns and cultural considerations. We looked at emotionally intelligent leadership from the angles of self, others and context. Now, we look at ourselves, our identities, and the beliefs we have in our abilities to navigate culturally foreign spaces. Bertrand Jones et al. (2016) stated, "Identity is our ever-evolving self-portrait (p.13). In many ways, this definition offers context to the earlier conversation on consciousness of self." As a culturally informed leader, context and environment are key factors in any understanding and awareness of one's core identities. Consider in your day-to-day interactions with peers, how often do you think about your national origin or your native language? For many, the answer is rarely, but when you spend time in another region of the world where the culture is vastly different, those identities (such as national origin and native language) can become quite apparent.

Abes et al. (2007) presented the model of multiple dimensions of identity development. The model showcases the fluidity of identity and how the salience of certain identities can shift based on context. In the example of national origin and native language, when you are in your home country and context, those identities may not be at the forefront of your mind. Take, for example, someone leaving the United States to study in Brazil, now, identities such as national origin and native language have become

TABLE 2.1	Interrelated Aspects of Culture
Aspect of Culture	**Consideration**
Government	What is happening in the region? Are their elections taking place? What are the sentiments from the general populous regarding the current regime? How does the government characteristics reflect the ideology and beliefs of the people?
Education	What is the value of education in the region? Is education available for all? What role do education institutions play in the shaping the local conversations? For example, in the United States, sports and collegiate athletics is a significant aspect of the educational and broader culture.
Religion	Religion can be both a faith-based and ethnic identity. What is the role that religion and faith play in the region? Are there observances that you may want to consider, and acknowledge as you work and lead in a global team? How do aspects of religion impact other aspects of culture (e.g. family, education marriage...)?
Marriage	Is marriage a major factor in the day-to-day lives of those in the region? How does the concept of marriage look similar (or differently) from that of your native country? What beliefs informed by religion and family shape the way marriage is viewed, described, and enacted in the region?
Family	Culturally, how does the role of family show up in the customs of the people in the region? How (if at all) does family impact the workplace of environment? When planning events with groups and teams, do extended family need to be considered in the planning of activities and events?
Medicine	Differences exist in healthcare from country-to-country. As you work in a region, consider what is the availability of health care (i.e. initiatives such as universal healthcare)? How does access to healthcare (or the lack thereof) impact the livelihood, well-being, and workings of those in the region?
Technology	Instagram, Tik-Tok, Facebook, artificial intelligence, smart-phones are all technological advances. These and so much more can influence how a society engages and the tone and tenor of a culture. What is the access and availability of technology in the region? Consider how technology is used within a region and how might it impact the ways in which you engage in groups and teams. Is the culture technological natives or late adopters?
Art	Music, film, and dance are just three of the numerous ways art is expressed. Reflect on your own culture, think about the core influencers in music, film, and dance and how their work has shaped contemporary culture where you live. Like leadership, culture is dynamic, meaning it is ever-changing. Your ability to be astute to the artistic influences of a region can have a significant impact on how you relate to the people within that community.

Source: Adapted from Ferraro (2009).

more prominent when thinking of being in Brazil with Portuguese as the majority language. As someone committed to leading in a global context, take time to consider your identities and how they shift in prominence based on environmental context. This is an important tool in developing a more accurate portrait of yourself.

You have a strong sense of your identity, and you have done the work to reflect on how context shifts the salience of your identities; now, let us turn our attention to the concept of efficacy. Dugan (2017) stated efficacy centers on our belief in ourselves to enact certain behaviors, and this belief (or lack thereof) in ourselves is a critical determinant in our overall leadership effectiveness and enactment. Have you considered your belief in your ability to successfully navigate a foreign culture? Beyond that, have you considered your belief in yourself to successfully navigate a foreign culture while leading a culturally/geographically diverse team? If you have never asked these questions, this is a good time to examine both.

Leadership is a process and so is efficacy. Efficacy is a domain that requires continuous work to forge, but as a leader, our self-belief is pre-determinate in our confidence in our ability to lead others. So, how does a person go about building their efficacy? Experiences such as engaging in opportunities to work in culturally diverse groups and teams, finding mentors who support you in your leadership development, and taking on new challenges and opportunities are key strategies to building you efficacy within yourself. The strength of our leadership efficacy comes from a host of factors, which are explored further in Chapter 3.

RESPONDING TO CULTURE SHOCK

You have considered your emotional intelligence, and you have given thought to who you are in the context of a foreign culture, now it is time to think about what lies ahead. Studying and working abroad can come with a great deal of excitement, the thought of experiencing new foods, cultures, and new ways of being can be an exhilarating prospect for many. One of the best ways to prepare is to be mindful of culture shock. First, let us explore the various symptoms of culture shock. Confusion over expected roles and behaviors is a common symptom of culture shock. Roles and behaviors can be in the formal and in the mundane—from how to effectively work in groups and teams, to simple gestures of hello. Recognizing the gestures and traditions you are accustomed to are not in alignment with the new culture you are experiencing can be a jarring experience. Secondly, there is a grief that can set in the loss of old and familiar surroundings. This can be in the inability to connect as regularly with friends and family, or not being able to get your favorite burger joint and pizzeria near your house. These feelings of loss are normal and can be expected especially when you are going to be abroad for a significant amount of time.

The challenges of navigating new norms, and the loss of familiar surroundings can leave people with lowered self-esteem, and feelings of homesickness that can lead to bouts of irritability, moodiness, and boredom (Ferraro & Broidy, 2017). Now, these symptoms are not shared to scare you, but to prepare you for what you may experience, and equip you with the understanding that if these symptoms arise, the feelings are normal and are to be expected.

To support you in the culture shock that may lie ahead, we present Table 2.2 the four stages of **culture shock** (Ferraro & Broidy, 2107; Oberg, 1960) and tips for navigating each stage.

Not everyone who goes abroad will find themselves traversing all four stages of culture shock. Some may be in a region for such a short period that they never leave the honeymoon stage, while others get so fraught with frustration and isolation that they remain stuck in stage two. Regardless of the stage you find yourself in, knowledge and awareness about what is to come is the key to successfully navigating and responding to the symptoms, feelings, and experiences of coming into a culture/geographic region with dynamic differences from that of your own.

TABLE 2.2 Stages of Culture Shock	
Stage of Culture	**Characteristics & Tips for Navigating**
Stage One: The Honeymoon	In this stage, attitudes and feelings about being in the new environment are generally positive. Stage one is marked by a sense of excitement and wonder as a person starts to navigate the new country. In this stage, remain open and curious, try new things, and start to observe the ways of the local community (e.g. consider trying public transportation, try new foods, be keen to current events impacting the region).
Stage Two: Irritation and Hostility	In stage two, challenges and problems begin to arise. The differences that at one point (typically during the honeymoon stage) seemed subtle between the host country and home are now distinct and noticeable. Stage two for many occurs after being in a region for several weeks or months. This stage is marked by feelings of frustration. It is during this stage you start to recognize the steep learning curve that can exist in learning the cultural norms of a foreign culture. During the stage, take note of your feelings, and recognize those moments of frustration (or defeat) where challenges seem to loom large. Stage two is a great time to reach out to family back home for support and to the community you have started to build in your host country to further aid you in learning how to navigate the new environment.

TABLE 2.2 Stages of Culture Shock (Continued)	
Stage of Culture	Characteristics & Tips for Navigating
Stage Three: Gradual Adjustment	This stage is the beginning of the arc of change in your perspective of the host country. You are starting to let go of your initial irritation and are beginning to find success in navigating the new cultural dynamics. The problems that seemed overwhelming and insurmountable (as noted in stage two) are now beginning to resolve themselves. In this stage, stay mindful of the strategies and tactics that have helped you move beyond some of the earlier challenges you experienced. Continue to take time to connect with natives of the community this might be through recreational activities or social outings—especially when traveling with others from your home country, be sure to take opportunities to break a way and continue to meet new people and explore new experiences. One of the greatest mistakes a person can make as the attempt to move from stage two to stage three is only engaging with people from their own country. In doing this, they risk further isolation and the learning/community that can form from continuing the "put yourself out there" in meeting and connecting with members of your host country community.
Stage Four: Biculturalism	This stage represents a full to near full integration into the new culture/region. In this stage, a person can successfully navigate the routine cultural functions (including greetings, manners of speech, etc.) and day-to-day activities of the region. Where stage two was marked by hostility, resistance, and loss, this stage is marked by openness and appreciation of the local customs and traditions of the host country. What was considered unsettling weeks/months ago is now welcomed and embraced. Stage four is a remarkable place to arrive and as a global leader, leaders should aspire to meet this moment in their journey. Often stage four needs to be met with reflection on considering what the return home will look like. Re-entry shock is a term used to label the experience of reverse culture shock (Niesen, 2010): where a person becomes so familiar with a new region that the return to the home country and culture comes with a shock in ways that mirror Stage Two.

Source: Adapted from Ferraro and Broidy (2107) and Oberg (1960).

STOP What are your initial reactions to the four stages of culture shock? What advice would you give someone at each of the various stages. Looking back on your own experiences, have there been moments in your life where you experienced a form of culture shock?

PUTTING THE PIECES TOGETHER

As you can see in Figure 2.1 shows, the pieces of the global puzzle are beginning to fill in to make a more complete picture. In this chapter, we honored that leadership starts with self, and as a culturally informed leader emotional intelligence, understanding of cultural contextual considerations and self-awareness are key drivers to success. In the spirit of acknowledging

Figure 2.1 Global Puzzle Pieces.

leadership starts with self, continue to be mindful of your identities, and how they present in various spaces. Remember, belief in yourself (efficacy), is important in the ways you grow your capacity to lead in globally diverse contexts. As you spend time abroad or engaging in an unfamiliar cultural context, keep in mind Ferraro's (2009) interrelated aspects of culture and consider how they serve as actors in how culture is displayed, enacted, and expressed. Finally, challenges, such as culture shock, are bound to present themselves, but the leader who honors that leadership first starts with self will be well equipped to handle what obstacles may come their way.

REFLECT ON YOUR OWN

- Who are you? What are your core values and how might both (who you are and your core values) inform your approach to culturally informed leadership?

- Reflection on the three pillars of emotional intelligence (consciousness of self, others and context) which of the three comes easiest for you and which is most difficult.
- How can understanding of Ferraro's (2009) interrelated aspects of culture be beneficial for the culturally informed leader?

REFLECT WITH A FRIEND

- What do you see as the key characteristics of the culturally informed leader?
- Who is someone you admire as a global leader? How do they practice the concepts of emotional intelligence as outlined within the chapter?
- What are some ways that others can support your efficacy and capacity as a global leader?

LEVELING UP!

Activity 1: Navigating Culture Shock

Rather than seeing culture shock as something to try to avoid, embrace it and work with it instead of against it. In this activity, work in a group to develop a skit where each of you play a character in the four stages of culture shock: Honeymoon, Irritation and Hostility, Gradual Adjustment, and Biculturalism. As a group, develop the context of where you are enacting the skit and use this as an opportunity to hone your improv skills. After several minutes of allowing the skit to play out, ask each other, how did it feel at the various stages of culture shock? For those in the earlier stages, what could others do to support you in progressing along? And for those in the latter stages of culture shock, what do you presume was needed to help you get there? Asking these questions and engaging this conversation may illuminate ways you need to be support and you can support others in successfully navigating foreign cultural terrain.

Activity 2: Who Are You?

The great leader is the self-aware leader. In this activity, take a piece of paper and start mapping out the events and the people in your life in chronological order. Map out those events, experiences, and moments that shaped your core values, beliefs, and positions. Beyond points in time, include those people (family, friends, teachers, etc.) who have shaped and informed who you are today. Once you have done this, go back and consider how those times and people have informed your cultural expressions. For example, in some households, everyone takes off their shoes before entering the house. In other traditions, the elders are greeted first when entering a space. Each experience and pivotal person in our lives shapes our cultural expressions. With greater awareness of our cultural traditions, we can have a greater appreciation of the traditions of others. By mapping out major events in your life, some of these cultural traditions may emerge and give you a greater sense of who you are.

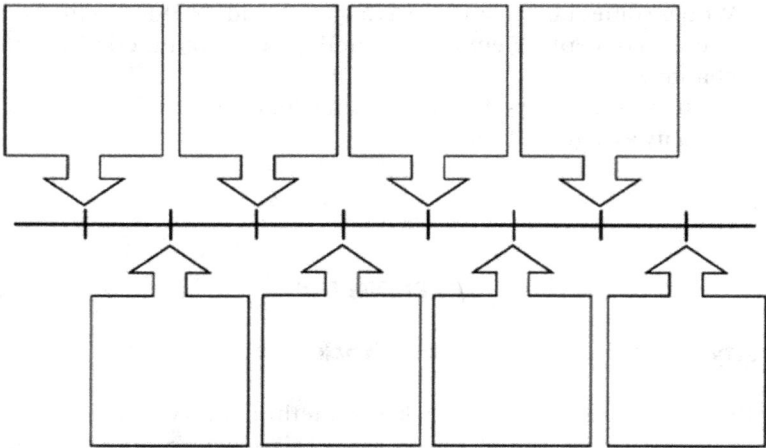

CHAPTER 3

SELF AS LEARNER

> Situating yourself as a learner in a new culture is critical in gaining the knowledge needed to not only engage with others daily, but to engage in the leadership process as both a leader and a follower. This chapter explores self as a learner and how you can embrace your leadership learning journey. It will highlight unconscious bias as well as the leadership learning model.

When entering various cultural contexts, approaching every situation as a learner is an accessible and humble way of being. We all have things to learn every single day. Even in a context in which you are familiar with, framing experiences and situations as opportunities to learn not only makes you more open, but it also allows for others to engage with you in more authentic ways. Situating yourself as a learner helps to put the pieces of the culturally informed leadership learning puzzle together (see Figure 3.1). In this chapter, you will think about yourself as a learner and how we often need to unlearn old ways and how to specifically learn leadership.

UNLEARNING AND RELEARNING

Situating yourself as a learner when you are in a different cultural context is essential to opening your head and heart to what you may learn. Oftentimes, it is critical to unlearn and relearn a different way of thinking, being, and doing. Nirenberg (2002) said having a cultural mindset is not always natural and can be hard to learn. We have all heard about **stereotypes;** it is

Considerations for Culturally Informed Leadership, pages 25–34
Copyright © 2026 by Emerald Publishing Limited
All rights of reproduction in any form reserved.
doi:10.1108/978-1-80592-469-220251004

when we think a member of a specific group to have certain characteristics without knowing them individually. **Unconscious bias** is the way stereotypes affect our understanding and behaviors in an unconscious way. These biases emerge and are acted upon without an individual's awareness or intention (Stanford, 2022). Some attributes of unconscious bias include that everyone has biases they are unaware of, these biases can be so engrained that you view them as truth, and these biases can influence attitudes and behaviors (Noon, 2018). At some point, we have all been affected, whether it was in a positive or negative way, from another's biased views of us. The collective influence of individual bias creates a larger system of bias. Reflecting on our own biases that occur unintentionally is critical when going to travel, visit, and study to a new culture.

To overcome the effects of unconscious bias it is important to intentionally reflect on our personal bias and how they came to be. One well known source of bias is that our brains naturally assign everything to a category to provide mental shortcuts, called schemas (Fiske & Taylor, 1991). Our families, upbringing, experiences with various social groups, whether that is direct or indirect experiences all influence our development of unconscious bias. All forms of media and how various groups are portrayed are also a large source of how unconscious biases form.

There are many types of bias that can show up as implicit or unintentional. By knowing what these specific biases are, it will assist in your reflection of bias you may hold and to unlearn them, especially when visiting a new cultural context. Turnbull (2016) provided some excellent definitions to several types of bias including:

- **Affinity bias** is our preference to be around people who are like us. This means we tend to choose those who look, act, or have similar backgrounds to us.
- **Assimilation bias** occurs when dominance is present and as a coping mechanism, others unconsciously change to fit in with the dominant culture.
- **Confirmation bias** is the inclination to seek out information confirming what we already believe and ignore information that is different from what we believe.
- **In-group bias** gives preferential treatment to those perceived to be members of our own group.
- **Pattern recognition bias** matches memories in which we see patters, even though those patterns may not exist.

Continuous unlearning our own biases and reflecting where they came from and how it influences our current thinking is critical. As you are unlearning these unconscious biases it allows you to relearn the beauty of various new cultures you get to experience.

LEADERSHIP LEARNING FRAMEWORK

As authors, one of our assumptions is that leadership can be learned. Specifically, being a leader is not something you are born with the ability to do. You learn how to engage in positive ways to influence others to work collectively toward creating positive change. Guthrie and Jenkins (2018; 2024) use the metaphor of a steering wheel in their leadership learning framework. The steering wheel visual (see Figure 3.1) demonstrates how we all need to guide, or steer, our own learning. Essentially, we have a responsibility to ourselves to not only engage in our own learning but steer it. We share the leadership learning framework (Guthrie & Jenkins, 2018) to pull back the curtain on how learning leadership can occur.

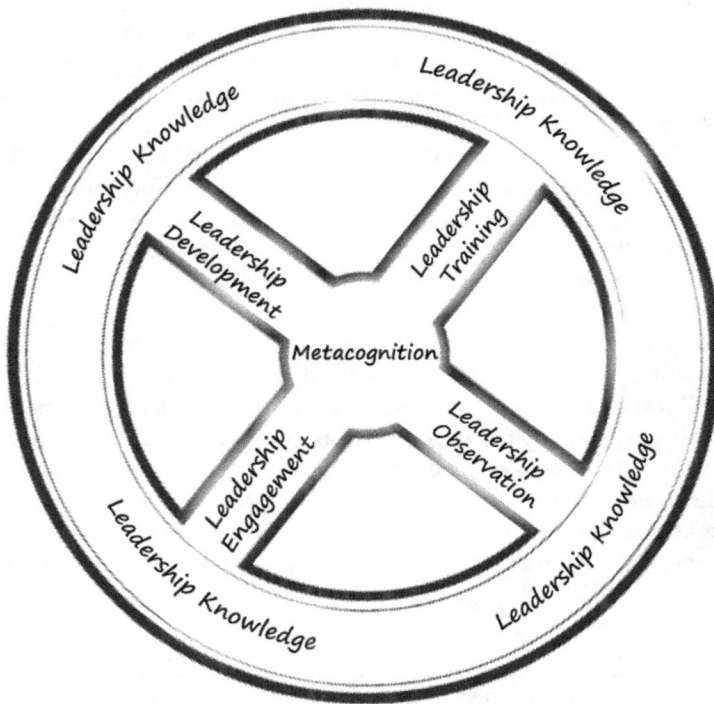

Figure 3.1 Leadership learning framework. *Source:* Reprinted from *Transforming Learning: The Role of Leadership Educators* (p. 58), by K. L. Guthrie and D. M. Jenkins, 2018, Information Age Publishing. Copyright 2018 by Information Age Publishing Inc. Reprinted with permission.

Working from the outside of the wheel to the middle, you can see leadership knowledge surrounds the entire wheel. Gaining knowledge of leadership concepts, theories, and skills is foundational and where leadership learning begins. We acquire leadership knowledge from various sources, and it starts with the language used by those around us to describe about leadership. There are four aspects connecting the outer ring of the wheel to the center. These aspects are leadership development, leadership training, leadership observation, and leadership engagement which all contribute to leadership metacognition at the center. Let's discuss the six aspects of leadership learning in more detail. The more you know, the more you can deeply engage in your own leadership learning. As we discuss these aspects, think about how you have learned leadership in the past and how you best learn leadership now. As you evolve as a person, so does the way you best learn and experience life.

Leadership knowledge is understood to be the "interdisciplinary, academic and applied field of study that focuses on the fluid process and components of the interaction between leaders and followers in a particular context" (Sowcik, 2012, p. 193). In the leadership learning journey, leadership knowledge is acquiring information and insights about the leadership process. To learn leadership knowledge is cognitive in nature and focuses on discovering new language, theories, concepts, and constructs related to leadership. Leadership knowledge is gained both in and out of the classroom including through community service opportunities, student organizations, and student employment. The focus of this book is leadership in various cultural contexts, so learning about leadership in different cultures is essential.

Leadership development is centered on the personal and intrapersonal elements of leadership learning, focused on the identity, needs, values, and readiness of the leader (Pontes & Weng, 2024; Rocco & Rupert Davis, 2024). This type of learning focuses on the person and considers their needs, values, readiness to lead, motivation to engage, identity, and other multiple dimensions of self. Human aspects of leadership learning may include knowledge and experiences with self-awareness, ethics, consciousness of self, citizenship, giving and receiving feedback, reflection, and others (Guthrie et al., 2021).

STOP What are 3–5 personal or interpersonal elements of leadership you hope to learn more about for your own personal development as a culturally informed leader? These human aspects could include (but not limited to) things such as self-awareness, feedback, empathy, empowerment, initiative, resilience, and others.

Leadership training can be understood as "the skill- and competency-based behavioral aspects of learning" often focused on mastery and/or behavioral change (Guthrie et al., 2021, p. 10). Focusing on skill development, this type of learning places a heavy emphasis on practicing on lessons and building upon them. With significant practice of skills and competencies learned in leadership, observable change in behavior can be seen. Leadership training may include topics on time management, facilitation of meetings, decision making, public speaking, giving feedback, active listening and so on.

Leadership observation is a "process focused on the cultural and social aspects of leadership learning" (Devies, 2022, p. 100) that lead to meaning-making reflection. In leadership observation, the learner is a passive recipient and leads to meaning-making reflection of what is seen. In this type of learning, the learner evaluates dynamics between participants in the leadership process, the power, privilege, inclusion, engagement, and inequity that is occurring. It is important to note that learning is culturally influenced, and the sociocultural context undergirds the observation and meaning making that comes from it (Guthrie & Jenkins, 2018).

STOP When have you observed leadership in the last week? Who were the leaders? Who were the followers? What was the context? What did you learn from observing the leadership process? How would you use observation techniques in a new cultural context to better understand leadership?

Leadership engagement is the involvement in "experiential, relational, interactional, and interpersonal aspects of leadership learning" (Guthrie & Jenkins, 2018, p. 67). Just like leadership observation, leadership engagement is created from the learner's experience. However, the learner is an active participant in leadership engagement. Meaning is constructed from learner's response from personal experiences with leadership (Risku & Holder, 2024). Many people are drawn to this type of learning. It is learning by doing. It is being an active participant. It is engaging in the process.

Finally, **leadership metacognition** is grounded in reflection, evaluation, and mindfulness to make sense of the learners' thoughts on their learning experiences (Guthrie & Jenkins, 2018, 2024). It is evaluative, analytical, adaptive, and complex. In leadership metacognition, the learner is critically aware and seeks to fully understand their thoughts about the process of leadership and the learning for leadership. Have you ever had an "ah-ha" moment? When several learning moments come together and bring a heightened level of awareness to the situation you are in? This is leadership metacognition.

LEADERSHIP IDENTITY, CAPACITY, AND EFFICACY

As seen in the culturally relevant leadership learning model (CRLL; Beatty & Guthrie, 2021; Bertrand Jones et al., 2016), leadership identity, capacity, and efficacy are pathways to leadership learning. Not only can one learn as an individual, but also from engaging in the process. This is critical in various cultural contexts when situating yourself as a learner. Let's talk about this further.

An individual's leadership identity development can show up in various ways through cultural contexts. One aspect to think about is how your nationality shows up in various cultures. If you grew up in the United States, how people view patriots can vary greatly, especially on a world stage. This is deeply rooted in cultural, social, and political histories of engagement. Being aware of how perceptions of power, authority, and even gender show up in different situations contribute to your leadership identity in various cultural contexts. One's capacity as a leader in various contexts is complex and nuanced. As Nirenberg (2002) pointed out, mastering the skills to navigate different cultures does not come naturally for most. This is something that you need to work on continuously. Always entering situations in different cultural contexts as a learner situates you as a humble participant rather than a person who claims to know everything. Dugan (2011) shared that capacity is also the synthesis and integration of experiences, attitudes, and information, which is the ability to lead in various cultural contexts. Connected to that, leadership efficacy development is something that one will continually need to reflect and stay in a space of learning. Especially in a cultural context that is not the one you were born into; it takes years of learning to believe you can successfully lead. As mentioned, identity, capacity, and efficacy are interrelated and to situate self as a learner in these areas within various cultural contexts is critical for positive interaction and acceptance.

PUTTING THE PIECES TOGETHER

In this chapter we focused on always situating ourselves as a learner, especially in various cultural contexts. Oftentimes we learn from stereotypes presented in media and different ways we are socialized; therefore, we need to unlearn and be open to relearning new information. This book will continue to build on being a learner by exploring how to be an engager and connecter as well, just as the global puzzle pieces continue to fill in (see Figure 3.2). Understanding what it means to be a learner, engager, and connecter is important to continuous growth as a culturally informed learner.

Figure 3.2 Global puzzle pieces.

REFLECT ON YOUR OWN

- Have you ever thought about how you learn leadership? What aspects of the leadership learning framework are you the most drawn to? Why?
- What specific cultural and leadership competencies do you want to learn to be a better leader in various cultural contexts?
- How can you foster a culture of continuous learning that is responsive to diverse cultural perspectives?

REFLECT WITH A FRIEND

- What are the unique challenges and opportunities for leadership learning in various cultural contexts?
- What are some ways you would intentionally learn about various cultures, cultural skills, and leadership in various cultural contexts?
- How can leadership development opportunities be created to maximize others to share their lived experiences as a source of learning and innovation? In other words, how would you create a leadership learning opportunity that centered on lived experiences that amplify various cultural experiences?

LEVELING UP!

Activity 1: Identifying Unconscious Bias

None of us want to intentionally be biased. However, every single one of us carries unconscious bias that we are often unaware of until we are honest with ourselves. It can be hard to genuinely reflect on what biases we hold and where they came from, but even harder to write them down or share them with others. For this activity, we encourage you to have courage to be honest in the name of unlearning and learning. Keep this private if that makes sense to you or share it with a friend; the important part is that you take the time to really dig deep. Remember, you may think of a bias as something good. For example, you may see a certain group of people being smart or always good dancers or athletic but can still be harmful to individuals associated with that group who might not possess those skills.

Write down at least two biases you may hold that includes the specific bias and who this bias is about. Next write down the source of where that bias possibly came from. For example, did you see this in media, through family, or by direct experiences. Finally, include specific strategies to reflect and become aware of when and how these unconscious biases are at play.

1. Identified Bias that Includes Specific Bias with Who:

   Possible Sources of Bias:

   Strategies to Increase Awareness of When and How these Emerge:

2. Identified Bias that Includes Specific Bias with Who:

   Possible Sources of Bias:

   Strategies to Increase Awareness of When and How these Emerge:

Activity 2: Intentional Leadership Learning

As the leadership learning framework (Guthrie & Jenkins, 2018) suggests, there are multiple ways of learning leadership. It is vital to be intentional in thinking about what you want to learn and steer your own leadership learning. In the table below, write down ways you will learn through the different aspects of the leadership learning framework. This could be how you will be more aware of this type of learning or how you will seek out to learn in this manner. For example, in leadership observation, you may choose to attend an event of a student organization you are not a part of. What can you learn about leadership through this type of observation?

Leadership Learning Aspect	Specific Way You Will Focus on This Learning
Leadership knowledge	
Leadership development	
Leadership training	
Leadership observation	
Leadership engagement	
Leadership metacognition	

Now, take one specific way listed above for each aspect and write it in the area of the steering wheel. Feel free to write on this page or sketch one in your notebook to write on. Once written, this will serve as your intentional plan for leadership learning in which you are steering. This plan will give you goals in which to strive for in your culturally informed leadership learning journey.

CHAPTER 4

SELF AS ENGAGER

> Sometimes the best way to learn is by doing. In this chapter, we look at leadership through the lens of engagement; that is outlining how one learns through direct interaction with their environment. The competencies of a global leader are offered to support your understanding of the skills required to effectively employ leadership principles in a foreign context. As you are reading, pay close attention to the ways you can put the concepts introduced into your leadership practice now and into the future.

In Chapter 3, we explored the six aspects of leadership learning (Guthrie & Jenkins, 2018, 2024). In this chapter, we dive deeper into two of those aspects of leadership learning: leadership engagement and leadership observation. Additionally, we will explore the competencies of a global leader (Osland, 2012) and offer considerations for expanding your global leadership context.

In many instances, leadership is a participative process. Meaning the best way to learn leadership is by doing it. Global leadership offers a similar vantage point for leadership that to be a leader in a global context; you must practice leadership in a cultural, geographical, and geopolitical environment that differs from your own. Secondly, (and some would argue more importantly) leadership in a global context requires observation. In other words, to lead effectively requires the ability to pay attention, be astute to your surroundings, and be observant of the ways people interact and engage with one another. Both aspects of leadership learning, leadership engagement, and leadership observation, require an understanding of self and self in the context of engager.

Considerations for Culturally Informed Leadership, pages 35–43
Copyright © 2026 by Emerald Publishing Limited
All rights of reproduction in any form reserved.
doi:10.1108/978-1-80592-469-220251005

The culturally informed leader must give attention to effective means of engagement in a foreign region. In Chapter 1, we covered the foundations of leadership. In many ways, global leadership has similarities to its domestic counterpart. A way to describe it is:

> Global leaders are individuals who effect significant positive change in organizations by building communities through the development of trust and the arrangement of organizations and process in a context involving multiple cross-boundary stakeholders, multiple sources of external cross-boundary authority and multiple cultures under conditions of temporal, geographic and cultural complexity (Mendehall et al., 2012, p. 20).

Global leadership showcases a greater concern for the interplay amongst people of different cultures rather than the effectiveness of one particular leadership approach/style.

COMPETENCIES OF A CULTURALLY INFORMED LEADER

The following competencies are taken from Osland's (2012) work on developing proficiencies as a global leader. As you read each of the competencies, consider how you would apply these in your leadership practice, where are your areas for growth, and who are the people to support you on your journey. The competencies are highlighted in bold. As you will see, the competencies of a global leader are reminiscent of those of any effective leader working and serving both domestically and abroad.

As you embark on your global leadership journey, remaining **open-minded** will be essential to your success. Each of us has considerations, traditions, and customs that are considered the norm in our day-to-day lives. When working, leading, and living in a culturally foreign region it is important to unbridle your preconceived notions of what is considered "normal" practice and allow yourself to be open to new ways of being, thinking, and living. The social, political, and cultural climate of another region is not there for us to judge, but for us to learn from. The best learning occurs when we remain open.

When traveling abroad, don't simply be a passive observer of the people, culture, and current events, but rather engage with an **active sense of curiosity**. The global leader takes time to learn customs, from how people greet one another to proper protocol when taking public transit. To possess cultural interest is to be open to moving beyond one's comfort zone, it means trying new things, experiencing new foods, and actively seeking opportunities that expose you to new practices. The sense of cultural curiosity should be complemented by sensitivity, be mindful of current events, and how people from a region perceive people from your place of origin. Consider how you will use technology to help support your learning. Use the knowledge you gain from this place of openness to inform how you engage and interact with others with whom you come into contact.

Life is complex and so are people; be aware of the "danger of the single story" (Adichie, 2009). The "single story" are those stereotypes we carry about a region, its people and the culture therein. Global leaders who possess the ability to **deal with complexity** understand that there are many dimensions and facets to a place. Ferraro (2009) states:

> Whenever dealing with any concept or generalization, such as the concept of culture it is important to avoid viewing it overly rigid or in a concrete way... generalization should be regarded as heuristic in nature, rather than as exact representations of reality (p. 41).

As a culturally informed leader, honor that within a region there are cultures within a culture, and no community is a monolith. As a leader, being nimble, open, and flexible are important traits to have.

As we discussed in Chapter 2, when looking at the various stages of culture shock (Ferraro & Broidy, 2017), adapting and adjusting to a foreign culture can be hard. As a culturally informed leader, identify the strategies that will help you live and thrive in the region you will be exploring. **Be resilient, resourceful, optimistic, and energetic;** these virtues will serve you well in your ability to thrive in a new cultural setting. Take time to reflect on what support you need to assist you in your adjustment. In your transition to an unfamiliar region, do not be afraid to ask for help. Remember, vulnerability is a form of strength in leadership, not weakness, and asking for what we need is a signifier of someone who is attuned to their leadership readiness.

The foundation of leadership is character. Global leaders are both open and ethical and **operate from a state of honesty and integrity**. As you are leading, think about the interests of others and avoid initiatives/decisions that are primarily self-serving. Move with courage in your interactions with others remaining clear about your core values and serve as a role model for others to do the same. Note, your job as a global leader is not to indoctrinate others to hold the same beliefs as you but to provide space where people can freely share their beliefs (as you share yours) with a common aim to advance the mission, vision, and values of the group, team, or organization.

Finally, whether at home or abroad, you need be mindful of your health and well-being. The mental stressors that can come in transition to a foreign culture can be significant. Feelings of isolation or loneliness and a decline in confidence in navigating a new region are all common side effects of culture shock (Ferraro & Broidy, 2017). As a global leader, consider what tools, such as therapy, family, and spiritual practice, can do to support your **personal stability** as you navigate what can sometimes be the rocky terrain of culturally acclimating to a new space. These competencies can serve as significant assets as you forge your path as a leader in a global context.

> **STOP** Reflect on how you currently work to develop the competencies highlighted by Osland (2012). Consider which competencies are strengths and which competencies are areas of growth on your leadership journey.

EXPANDING YOUR GLOBAL CONTEXT

The dearth of leaders with global experiences, perspectives, and context is a gap that causes concerns for many corporations working in an international context (Ng et al., 2009). As you look to grow as a culturally informed leader, consider how you are mindful of your limitations in considering multiple cultural contexts and the potential shortcomings of leaders working within global industries. Commit to being a leader who stays curious and globally minded, here are suggested action steps to continue to cultivate that skill set.

First, consider how you can gain concrete experiences that allow you to develop your skills as a global leader. Note, you do not have to visit a different region to grow in your skills as a global leader. With advancements in technology, collaboration, and community building with others from different parts of the world can be successful virtually. Second, when available, consider opportunities like studying or interning abroad that allow you first-hand opportunities to grow and apply your cultural knowledge in a particular region. If you are not able to go abroad, take opportunities to learn from cultural experiences that are different from your own in your local area. If you live in a city with diverse cultural centers, try spending time in neighborhoods that allow you to internally reflect on your own observations, feelings and assumptions.

For those who have friends and family from other regions of the world, consider those moments where you have made cultural missteps. Perhaps it was not taking off your shoes when you enter a home, not waiting for the eldest in the family to be served first, or greeting with a handshake when the cultural salutation is different. Whenever you experience these moments, reflect and observe. Reflect on your actions, observe how your actions were received, and identify the learning that is there for you in this experience. This is what leadership educators call metacognition (Guthrie and Jenkins, 2018); these are opportunities where one intentionally reflects on the learning that comes from an experience and how that learning can be applied to effective practices in the future. Finally, culture is dynamic (ever-changing), as a culturally informed leader, commit yourself to being a lifelong learner.

In many culturally diverse situations, the "right" approach is not always going to be explicitly evident. Being able to navigate situations that are not black and white, and require intellectual examination and reflection are points to strengthen as you dedicate yourself to grow your ability to lead in a cross-cultural context. Lastly, in this idea of expanding your global context, take opportunities to actively test and experiment with your global cultural learning. For some, this may look like downloading an application on your phone that aids in learning a new language. As you learn the new skills, actively experiment with your abilities in safe and appropriate environments. Remember, as you continue to grow as a global leader, often the best way to learn is by active experimentation.

STOP

In culturally informed leadership, communication patterns matter. Consider how the culturally informed leader may need to adjust their communication style based on high versus low context. What are some strategies or tools you can think of that can aid you in shifting your contextual communication patterns?

CONSIDERATIONS FOR PRACTICE

This chapter opened with a revisit of two of the six aspects of leadership learning (leadership engagement and leadership observation). We then explored the various competencies of being a global leader and ways to expand your global context. Now, let us take a moment and showcase practical ways you can grow your competence and expand your global context. Each of us has those aspects about ourselves known by others, but not known by us. It is like having something stuck in your teeth. Others know, but you may not be aware yourself. Like when you have something stuck in your teeth, ask someone about your leadership.

Confide in those you trust about your commitment to grow in your cultural curiosity as a leader. Ask those around you how they perceive you in being open-minded and culturally astute. Talk with mentors and friends about on ways you can continue to grow your cultural curiosity and sensitivity to cultural differences with more open-mindedness and less judgment.

Earlier in the chapter, we discussed the "danger in the single story" (Adichie, 2009) and how stereotypes can burden us with preconceived notions of other cultures with limited basis in facts. As a person committed to global leadership, start to ask yourself, "What are some of the biases I hold about communities/cultures/groups that differ from mine?" Asking the sometimes hard, uncomfortable, but important questions can begin to unbridle the broad-brush stroke assumptions that can be made about a community. When we engage in this work, we start to see people, communities, and cultures with greater levels of complexity, understanding, and awareness.

As we have said before, leadership is a process and as a process, it is something that we will continue to revisit, find success, and at times meet with failure throughout our lifetime. In global leadership, there will be many times that one falters, makes cultural missteps and fall short of the goal. Do not let mistakes along the way deter you or meet you in a spirit of defeat. Rather, employ the leadership learning aspect of metacognition (see Chapter 3) where you take each moment and examine the learning that is there for you. Now, in your day-to-day interactions, start to reflect and journal about the learning that each day presents. When done regularly (as part of a daily practice) journaling can become a catalog of the various insights and lessons learned along the path to serving and leading in a global context.

Finally, as you think of yourself as an engager in global leadership, be keen to ground all your actions and intentions in integrity. The keystone for leadership success is integrity. Be true to yourself and as a consequence, be true to others. As you continue on the path to culturally informed leadership, examine your intentions, consider the ways you work to build trust, and the ways you move with a practice that builds meaningful interactions and authentic connections.

PUTTING THE PIECES TOGETHER

In this chapter, we offered recommendations for building your competency as a culturally informed leader. With Osland's (2012) proficiencies of a global leader as a frame, you are supported with the tools to effectively engage in another region of the world. We took this opportunity to once again highlight that being a culturally informed leader comes with ambiguity and not every decision will come with black and white/right or wrong options to consider. As a leader, be someone who engages in curiosity, who moves with openness, and works to cultivate trusting relationships. The leader who accomplishes those tasks will be well on their way to putting the right pieces in place on the puzzle board of culturally informed leadership. As you can see in Figure 4.1, the puzzle pieces continue to fill in creating a more complete picture.

REFLECT ON YOUR OWN

- As you consider the global competencies outlined in this chapter, which stand out for you?

Figure 4.1 Global puzzle pieces.

- Which of the global competencies do you feel most proficient, which do you feel are the greatest areas for growth?
- Right now, what are some of the ways you can continue to expand your context as a global leader?

REFLECT WITH A FRIEND

- With a friend, consider a country with a cultural context that is different than your own. In your conversation discuss the following:
  - What practical strategies would you employ to strengthen your global competencies when working/leading in this context?

- What are some of the assumptions/stereotypes associated with the region?
- How would you consult someone looking to deconstruct the assumptions/stereotypes held toward people in the region?
- Allow this conversation and the points made to be a simulation of how you will have critical and reflective conversations in future experiences as you consider your leadership in a particular region.
- Context matters. In this chapter, we discussed low vs high context cultures, what do you consider to be some of the mistakes that potentially could be made by someone who is coming from a low context culture for someone working in high context culture?

LEVELING UP!

Activity 1: Curating Your Leadership Council

In the table provided below, start to consider who are the people you will consult with about those aspects of yourself that you may not be aware of and knowledge about could support you as a culturally informed leader. Consider your rationale for reaching out to each of them and think about the questions you want to pose to them. Be sure to tailor your questions to each person and remember this does not have to be someone you deem a culturally informed leader, but someone who can speak to those aspects of yourself such as cultural sensitivity and curiosity, which are essential to effective leadership.

Name	Rationale	Question Posed	Response

Activity 2: The Pitfall of the "Single Story" Narrative

Take 20 minutes to watch Chimamanda Adichie's Ted Talk on the Danger of the Single Story (you can find the video by doing a Google search for "Danger of the Single Story). As you watch the video, reflect on the following questions:

- What are some of the "single stories" you have developed about a region or a group of people?
- What (and who) supported the "single stories" you have developed about others?
- In what ways can you begin to reflect on your own biases and the stereotypes they help propagate

CHAPTER 5

SELF AS CONNECTOR

Self as Connector delves into connecting past and present experiences to culturally informed leadership. Included is a discussion on cultural inclusion, mindfulness, and authenticity and how all three play a role in the context of cross-cultural leadership.

In this chapter, we look to connect our understanding of self as a learner, with engager, and bring those together into application. As a culturally informed leader, your goal is to be cosmopolitan. This is a person "who can integrate and cross-fertilize knowledge and manage dispersed centers of expertise, influence, and production (Osland, 2012, p. 45). Being a cosmopolitan leader calls on you to tie together your previous experiences to navigate new circumstances and environments. The cosmopolitan leader is one who actively works to diversify their involvements, build their cognitive and emotional flexibility, and invokes a leadership approach that is expansive rather than insular (Gundling & Williams, 2021).

A distinction between culturally informed leadership and its domestic counterpart is the ability to work and lead across diverse cultural settings (Lane & Maznevski, 2014). In a world deeply impacted by globalization, cultures are diverging and converging simultaneously. As a leader, it is important to recognize the growth in technology, the importance of relationships, and the inherent connectedness of individuals across cultures.

We understand not everyone will have the availability to travel and/or study abroad, but you can start looking at your experiences now and see how they can apply to global leadership. We invite you to reflect on the various

Considerations for Culturally Informed Leadership, pages 45–55
Copyright © 2026 by Emerald Publishing Limited
doi:10.1108/978-1-80592-469-220251008

transitions in your life. Think about the things you observed in those settings. For instance, in your transition to college or a new job, what were the cultural symbols you observed? This could be in your college mascot, the way people participate in collegiate sporting events, or on a job, experiencing the first team meeting with your colleagues in the office. Additionally, consider those times you felt excluded, where you lacked a sense of belonging those spaces of reflection can serve to not only give you empathy in the transition of others but also awareness of the tools that support your transition, community building, and engagement. Gundling and Williams (2021) state, "leaders must draw upon their own upbringing and core values while being deliberately open to mind-blowing experiences with colleagues from different backgrounds that could change them forever" (p. 198). Reflecting on your own experiences can serve as a good tool in preparing to transition into a space that will gauge your cross-cultural aptitude.

ARC OF NAVIGATING TRANSITIONS

Life is full of transitions and working and leading abroad is one of the many transitions one may experience in life. Dr. Nancy Schlossberg offers a four "S" approach to think about transitions (as cited in Patton et al., 2016). First is the **situation**. Think back on a moment of transition in your own life. For the premise of this example, we will go back to the transition to college or to a new job. How did that transition feel? What made the transition easy? What made the transition difficult? Second are the **strategies**. Again, ask yourself key questions: What strategies did I use to guide my transition to college? For some, the strategy included being involved in a club and organization, for others, it was connecting with students on campus who could assist you navigate the transition. The third "S" is **support**. Looking back to the start of college, who were the supports in your life? What role did family, friends, and loved ones play in aiding in your transition? The final "S" (and we have spoken to this before) is **self**. What was your confidence level going into the transition to college? What were your beliefs in your skills and abilities to successfully navigate college? The questions we invite you to consider are helpful for any leader looking to navigate transitions powerfully, mindfully, and intentionally. These four areas: situation, strategies, support, and self are pivotal when contemplating your transition as a student studying abroad or as a leader working/serving in a foreign region.

| STOP | Now that we have explored the four "S" of transition, think of a specific example of transition in your own life. Place each of the "S" in that transition. What did you learn in that change that might apply to thinking about transition in a culturally foreign context? |

Keep in mind, we are often using confirmation bias as our meaning-making for the world. This is where we shape our expectations and assumptions based on previous lived experiences (Gundling & Williams, 2021). While confirmation bias can be helpful in some regards, it can pose several vulnerabilities in a leader's ability to successfully navigate the transition from one cultural context to another.

Let us take a deeper look specifically at strategies that contribute to the success of a global leader. First, remember what we shared in Chapter 2 on the four stages of culture shock: honeymoon, irritation/hostility, gradual adjustment, and biculturalism (Ferraro & Broidy, 2017). Reminding yourself of these four stages of culture shock can be a helpful resource for self-validation when challenging emotions come up for you—knowing that it is a part of the process of overcoming the difficulties in adjusting to a new cultural context.

Del Vitto (2008) found two of the leading causes for expatriates to leave a job assignment in another country are because of poor quality of life and an inability to adapt. When someone goes to work (or study) abroad, they are often met with feelings of isolation and homesickness. To confront some of the feelings of isolation (as you are able), get involved in the local community. If you enjoy physical activity, consider getting involved in recreational sports leagues. As an alumnus, consider contacting your college/university alumni association and inquiring about what alumni chapters/clubs the institution has abroad. In your involvement with those local to the region, be open, engage in active listening, and be intentional in your outreach to others with differing and diverse perspectives (Gundling & Williams, 2021). Consider about volunteering in the local community and use that to network and build in the new region you now call home. Whether it is getting involved in a sports league, an alumni chapter, or volunteering, each of these strategies to combat the challenges of being abroad can be helpful in not only building community but also learning and observing the local customs, traditions, and culture of the region. As a culturally informed leader, your involvement in the local community will support feelings of belonging and strengthen your resilience (a key component of global leadership, as discussed in Chapter 4).

Connections are key. As a culturally informed leader, be present to the ways you curate a diverse network of people who have an understanding and knowledge about the region (Osland, 2012). Take note of ways your networks and the community can assist you in gaining knowledge beneficial in your ability to navigate the spaces and places you work and lead. As you try to build connections, keep the following in mind-be open and flexible, move with integrity (and authenticity) in developing connections, and in the community, seek out individuals who not only can provide you with an understanding of the region, but also the emotional/communal support that is often essential to maneuvering another region of the world.

Keeping with the strategies shared before, one additional recommendation is to be aware and mindful of the place you will be working (or studying abroad). Awareness is knowing the current social and political landscape of places and spaces in the region you will be in. Safety and security concerns (that often stem from geopolitical situations in the region) are one of the major stressors for those working abroad. Before visiting (or moving) to a region, familiarize yourself with current happenings in the area. What are the local concerns? What are the safety considerations? What are the economic points of discussion? Questions like these places the culturally informed leader in a powerful position to not only navigate but also thrive in the transition from moving from one country to another.

MINDFULNESS AND A CULTURALLY INFORMED LEADER

Leaders who are unaware (or mindless) to the nuances of culture and the differences between one culture to another do so at the risk of not being able to build strong connections with others. Thomas and Inkson (2017) speak to the concept of mindfulness in three ways: **mindful attention**, **mindful monitoring**, and **mindful regulation**. Mindful attention asks us to consider our own biases (those that are conscious and unconscious), assumptions, ideas and emotions. Mindful attention goes back to our earlier conversations in Chapter 4 where we discussed observation. Mindful attention is taking in your surroundings and asking yourself, what am noticing in others' expressions? What am I hearing (in communication tone and tenor)? Furthermore, examine your communication patterns and how you are adapting those patterns to your new environment. Mindful attention is a great teacher for inquisitive leaders dedicated to acclimating themselves to a foreign culture.

The second form of mindfulness is mindful monitoring Mindful monitoring connects back to the conversations in Chapter 2 around self-awareness. Remember, "self-awareness is a contact sport, and biases are readily aroused when people come into contact with others from different backgrounds" (Gundling & Williams, 2021, p. 123). The leader who mindfully monitors will ask themselves proactively, where am I at this point in my culture acclimation?…am I am in the earlier stages such as the honeymoon, or have I progressed further to gradual adjustment/biculturalism? In this practice of mindfulness, think of those things that may limit you: stubbornness, inconsistency of behavior, inability to find common ground with others etc.; these behaviors mitigated can aid in building connections with others. Mindful monitoring equips the culturally informed leader to powerfully employ strategies and supports when needed.

The third form of mindfulness is mindful regulation. Mindful regulation is the art of knowing when to respond and when a response is not necessary. This form of mindfulness is about honoring when additional information is needed to either affirm or reject previous understandings held. Mindful regulation connects to earlier conversations (see Chapter 2) on emotional intelligence (EI). Like EI, a leader who can mindfully regulate is well suited to build healthy and productive partnerships in a cross-cultural context, because they are able to monitor their emotions and respond to situations accordingly. Mindfulness is a dynamic step in building strong connections with others. A mindful, culturally informed leader can communicate and interact powerfully with people of diverse backgrounds and cultures. In doing this mindfulness work, not only are you building your awareness of others, but also your ability to accurately make judgments about culturally diverse ways of working, communicating, and engaging.

> **STOP**
>
> Take time to look at your own mindfulness practices. How do you engage in mindful exercises? Consider what cultural faux pas can be made when a leader does not practice mindfulness regularly. How do you see mindfulness connecting to the concept of emotional intelligent leadership (highlighted in Chapter 2).

AUTHENTICITY AS A TOOL

You have taken time to reflect on your experiences and connect them to your new cultural environment. Additionally, you have centered yourself in mindful practices with the intent of being aware of yourself, your environment, and your context. Now, consider how you practice both with attention given to **authenticity**.

Authenticity is a contemporary theory of leadership. Those who practice authentic leadership have a strong sense of purpose and clarity about what is right and what is wrong, they build strong and trusting relationships with others, they stay true to (and act upon) their core values, and they are empathetic to the plight of others (Northouse, 2022). The argument can be made that these virtues of authenticity can employed across diverse contexts both domestically and abroad, but how those virtues are expressed may look differently.

Authenticity is articulated differently across cultures and regions (Moreno & Kolouris, 2017). For example, in some cultures (e.g. United States, Canada, and Australia), storytelling is an effective way to demonstrate authenticity. In these regions, storytelling allows people to share with others details about themselves, their journey, and the experiences that make them who they are. Through storytelling (in certain regions), people build connections with others, establish trust, and exhibit a level of authenticity that can support establishing relationships and rapport with others. Through storytelling, leaders can foster a sense of in-group belonging and deeper connections. While personal narratives can be rich and beneficial, "leaders must learn to balance storytelling with story-asking" (Gundling & Williams, 2021, p. 221). Conversely, in regions such as China, Japan, and Vietnam, storytelling does not illustrate authenticity. Instead, storytelling is seen as self-absorbed and limiting in its availability to serve as a relationship builder with others. Understanding that authenticity looks different across cultures is incredibly important. For authenticity to be conveyed effectively, one must have a strong and rich understanding of the cultural context in which they are working, leading, and serving.

THE LOOKING GLASS OF A CULTURALLY INFORMED LEADER

Like with authenticity, our upbringing and cultural lens color how we see and experience people, places, and events. As a leader who moves with openness, consider the lens through which you view the world and how it shapes your judgments. Aspects of culture, such as politics, social issues, and human liberties, look different from region to region. As a leader committed to openness, you are advised to go into spaces with curiosity instead of judgment. This can be challenging when the customs, practices, and liberties you are used to look completely different from the those of the region you are studying, working or leading. In those situations where culturally differences are prominent, remember truths and perspectives are not universal. Lane and Maznevski (2014) call the perspectives and meaning making we develop from our interactions/observations of another our "looking glass." The looking glass is what has us judge one's acts as normal and another's acts as otherworldly. Our perspectives (or looking glass) come from our culture.

Ethnocentrism "is the tendency for people to evaluate a foreigner's behavior by the standards of their own culture, which they believe is superior to all others. ...[it is] our own culture that we assume to be correct, and all others are wrong or at the very least strange (Ferraro, 2009, p. 41). Ethnocentrism comes out of our reliance of holding another's culture in comparison of our own with the belief that our own culture is superior to that of others (Ferraro, 2009). Our cultural traditions form our assumptions, beliefs, and values. Our culture is what gives us the belief and understanding of how we should and should not engage with others. Our culture has us shake hands in one society and bow in another; our culture has us tip for good service in one society and simply say thank you in another; our culture gives us the blueprint for belonging in the society in which we live.

A person becomes much more aware of their own culture when they are in the culture of another. But awareness alone is not enough, this must be met with action (Gundling & Williams, 2021). The more exposure one has to cultures and traditions other than their own, the less likely they are to be close-minded to the practices of others. Through exposure to culturally diverse spaces, leaders strengthen their capacity to lead and serve in international settings (Osland, 2012). Nirenberg (2002) states:

> One needs to appreciate the cultural differences, not just differences in conversation regarding how work gets done – but people's underlying belief and behavior systems. In building relations it is important to become inter-culturally fluent – able to relate to people no matter where you meet them, and more important for the [culturally-informed] leader, work with them toward the accomplishment of mutual goals (p. 17).

At the center of the notion of "self as connector" is an inherent belief in inclusion. Inclusive leadership is relevant to all who seek to build connections with others. Like other concepts within this chapter, inclusion is culture-bound and culture-specific. As a leader who is committed to culturally informed leadership, withhold judgment of another region's culture. Instead, critically examine your capacity to be in spaces and places where truths, liberties, and freedoms look (and/or are perceived) differently from your cultural context. As you observe cultures different than your own, consider this acronym developed by Lane and Maznevski (2014), D.I.E.: Describe, Interpret, Evaluate. First, **describe**; consider the words you use to talk about foreign culture. Reflect on the assumptions made and how those color your description. Second, **interpret**; in your observations of everything from casual greetings to nonverbal gestures, to faith practices, consider the ways you interpret experiences and how those interpretations are based on the subjectiveness of your own experiences. Finally, **evaluate**; when experiencing a foreign culture, give yourself time and space to formulate multiple interpretations and multiple perspectives.

Engaging in this work of connecting past experiences, with current cultural context is not always easy and it requires integrity. Integrity is the integration and consistent practice of your beliefs, what you say, and how you behave. Integrity is at the heart of leadership and foregrounds our ability to build trust and ultimately connection with others. Our integrity and clarity of our own values, need to be matched with an awareness that values (and specifically ethics) are not defined the same (universally) across cultures.

Be firm in your integrity and clear about your values and how your values inform your choices and the ways you engage with others (Lane & Maznevski, 2014). The culturally informed leader must move with flexibility in their ethical perspectives in order to sustain connection with others (Ting & Toomey, 2012). In other words, like with other aspects of culture, judge another's ethics not by your own cultural context, but based on the awareness you draw from the experiences and interactions you have with others. Ethics and integrity are two concepts we have explored throughout this book, and here as we speak the looking glass of the culturally informed leader, it is important to reinforce those concepts here.

As a leader, allow the multiplicity of considerations you collect to shape the way you evaluate the culture of another. Culture, ethics, and societal norms do not come in uniform packaging. Rather, what comprises culture is a set of dynamic, complex, and interrelated considerations. These various factors form how culture moves, is shaped, and expressed. As you work to build connections, remain mindful of the diversity within your community. Take initiative to cultivate diversity and inclusion in the spaces you work, lead, and live (Gundling & Williams, 2021). Remember, the leader who can unbridle their judgments of another's culture and view cultural (and ethical) differences with appreciation rather than judgment is the leader who is truly and authentically fashioned to work and collaborate in geo and socio-politically diverse spaces.

PUTTING THE PIECES TOGETHER

We turn the discussion from being a learner and an engager, to being a connector. As seen in Figure 5.1, the global puzzle pieces continue to show us a more complete picture of being a culturally informed leader. In this chapter, we explored strategies and tactics for building community and strengthening your resilience as you successfully navigate the transition of being in a foreign cultural community. The work from Thomas and Inkson (2017) gave us language for thinking about how to practice mindfulness in three areas: attention, monitoring, and regulation. We are reminded that authenticity while good for building connections is expressed differently from culture to culture and as a leader being mindful of those differences is key. Finally, through each aspect of relationship building and cultural exploration, continue to foster your understanding (and appreciation) for diversity. Be keen not to over generalize or to allow ethnocentric tendencies cast judgment of another group. Instead, as we have discussed throughout this book, move with openness and curiosity. You might be surprised about what you learn not only about another region, but also about yourself as you hone your ability to see yourself as a connector.

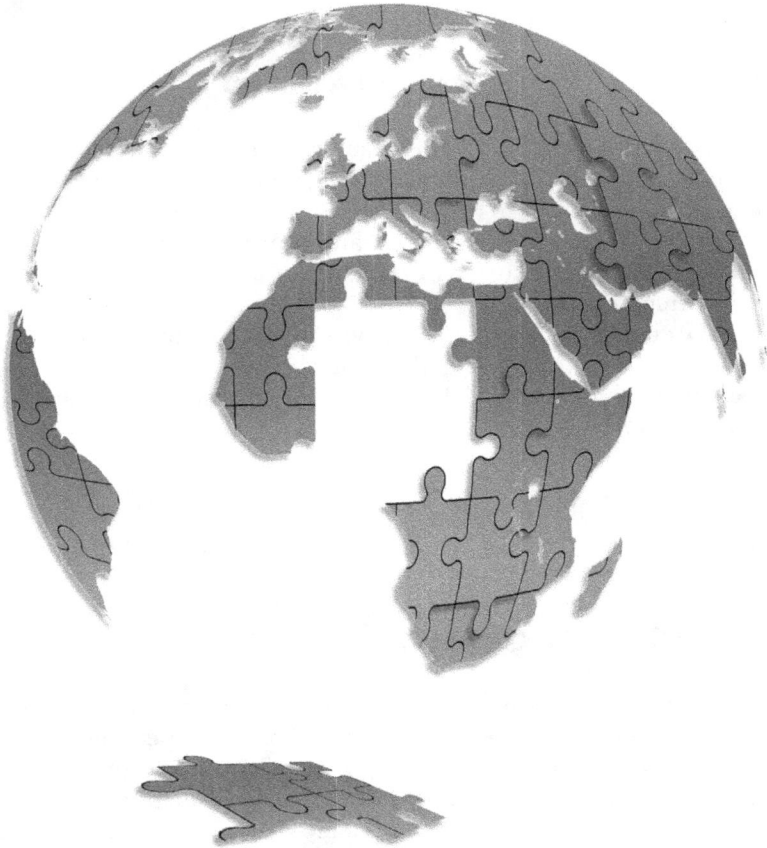

Figure 5.1 Global puzzle pieces.

REFLECT ON YOUR OWN

- Identify three ways you can connect your personal experiences of navigating a new environment to what is required for the culturally informed leader working in a foreign environment.
- Consider your own thoughts and reactions to the discussion on storytelling as a conveyor of authenticity. How have you used or seen it used by others), the concept of storytelling used to portray authenticity? How might storytelling be ineffective in presenting authenticity?
- How do you see the topic of connection across cultures linked to elements of diversity and inclusion within leadership development?

REFLECT WITH A FRIEND

- Reflect on your communities (family, friends, etc.) how does your community of family and peers reflect the type of diversity and inclusion inherent in culturally informed leadership?
- How do you actively work to expand your connections and diversify your peer community? Why is this important to being a culturally informed leader?
- How do you practice authenticity? How do you know others are being authentic with you? How might culture inform how authenticity is seen and received in one region that might look different in another?

LEVELING UP!

Activity 1: Make the Connection

In this chapter, we discuss reflecting on your past experiences and considering how they have shaped and informed your perspectives on culture and how you can connect these perspectives with leadership. With this activity, think of two distinct experiences that have shaped your cultural perspective in leadership. Perhaps, it is a moment growing up and interactions with loved ones that informed your understanding of community and of family. Conversely, it could have been an experience where you noticed a culture different from your own—for example, you observed how people interacted with servers in a restaurant. Think back on two experiences that informed your understanding of culture and then consider the following questions:

- What did the experience teach you about culture?
- In the examples you identified who were the people, what were the spaces, and how engagement with both informed you of the culture.
- What biases may you have based on what you learned about culture from other experiences?
- How will you work to honor your cultural understandings while simultaneously not judging other's understanding based on differing cultural contexts? Does any of these perspectives inform how you view leadership in various cultural contexts?

Activity 2: The Culture Soundtrack

The arts are a large part of the culture (Ferraro, 2009) and leadership (Guthrie & Jenkins, 2018), they can transmit the values, beliefs, and guiding principles of a society and provide opportunities to learn about leadership. In this activity, you are asked to develop a cultural soundtrack. Identify 10 songs, perhaps these are personal favorites from your streaming playlist or songs that invoke memories from childhood. With this activity, keep as a reminder, the role media and arts play in shaping and articulating culture; as you develop this soundtrack, ask yourself the following:

- What was the context (the year, era in history, etc.) in which the song was developed?
- How does this song convey about culture?
- What can a person who listens to this song infer about the community where the music derives?
- What does this song tell you about the values and beliefs of the listener? Are there lessons about leadership in these songs?
- In your experience, how have you seen music shape, inform, and tell the story of a society's culture? What lessons in here relate to being a culturally informed leader?

Your reflection on your own cultural soundtrack can give you insights on how to observe (through the arts) a cultural soundtrack different from your own and how this relates to leadership and connects to being a culturally informed leader.

CHAPTER 6

EMBRACING THE JOURNEY

> Throughout this book you have been reflecting on what it means to be a culturally informed leader. This chapter explores being a learner, engager, and connecter simultaneously to thrive not only in your culturally informed leadership learning journey, but as you learn, engage, and connect in life.

In this book, you explored how YOU can show up in various cultural contexts. As we have mentioned, you chose how to show up in various situations. To show up as a learner first has significant impact not only on your own learning but becoming a true engager in the world. This book helped you explore the process of leadership, which includes the context, leader, and follower (remember the triangle in Chapter 1?). We shared the progression of culturally informed leadership learning (see Figure 6.1) in which Chapter 2 helped you explore self-understanding, Chapter 3 discussed how we can lean into learning, Chapter 4 shared how we can focus on engaging with diverse cultures, and Chapter 5 celebrates how we can connect culture and ideas to the process of leadership.

Now that we have explored these areas of learner, engager, and connector, it is time to think about what it means to be a culturally informed leader.

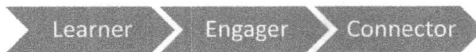

Learner ⟩ Engager ⟩ Connector

Figure 6.1 Progression of culturally informed leadership learning.

Considerations for Culturally Informed Leadership, pages 57–65
Copyright © 2026 by Emerald Publishing Limited
All rights of reproduction in any form reserved.
doi:10.1108/978-1-80592-469-220251007

BEING A CULTURALLY INFORMED LEADER

This entire book has been about how to be a culturally informed leader. As we reminded you above, we encourage you to be a learner, engager, and a connector. We presented this as a progression, because learning before you engage is important. You also need to engage before you make connections with people, ideas, and things. However, it is important to keep learning, engaging, and connecting simultaneously. Each day we have opportunities to learn, if we stop and listen. We have opportunities to engage with others if we intentionally pause and participate with others. This could be a smile, a brief conversation, or showing up.

Fully embracing the journey of being a culturally informed leader means honoring and acknowledging the complexities that come with learning, engaging, and connecting in various cultural contexts. There are a lot of differences and honestly, nuances, when considering various cultural contexts, especially when being socialized in a Western context. So often, our social construction of what leadership *should* look like is solely based on our lens that only developed with learning, integration, and socialization in the United States. Although the United States is made up of diverse people, culture context from around the world gets lost. Striving to be a culturally informed leader is being a learner first, then intentionally engaging in the cultural context you are in. Making the connections to current situations in various cultural contexts help you become and be a culturally informed leader. A critical component of being a culturally informed leader is to focus on ways to thrive, which means continuously develop, and help those around you thrive.

THRIVING AS A WAY OF BEING

You may ask yourself-what does it mean to thrive? How can I thrive more and stop just surviving? Thriving refers to the process of growing and developing in a way that leads to a more positive overall well-being (Seligman, 2011). Another way to describe thriving, how we like to say it, is evolving energetically. What a cool thing to not only think about, but to BE about. Evolving energetically. Being better with energy.

Thriving focuses on the journey. It emphasizes resilience, improvement, and adaptability in various aspects of life. Thriving is the ability to overcome challenges, grow stronger, and adapt to changes. In short, thriving is about being the best version of yourself, despite any challenges that may come your way, and continue to make progress toward your goals.

Oftentimes thriving and flourishing are used interchangeably, but they are slightly different concepts. As mentioned, thriving is a process of growth; however, flourishing is about arriving at a state of well-being.

Thriving is about adapting and flourishing is about functioning at a specific level and reaching fulfillment. Thriving is about resilience, being able to grow through challenges where flourishing is about achieving balance in all parts of your life. Overall thriving is about the journey of growth and flourishing is about the destination where an individual is in a state of well-being and fulfillment.

Now, think about thriving and flourishing as it relates to being a culturally informed leader. If we situate ourselves as a learner, engager, and connector in cultural contexts unfamiliar to us, we will constantly adapt to the new experiences we encounter. Even by the adaption to new situations, we are engaging in continuous growth. Eventually, focus will shift toward focusing on achieving balance in different areas of your life leading to fulfillment and well-being.

> **STOP** Let's pause here. How are you feeling? Do you feel like you are in a state of thriving? Or do you think you are more in a state of surviving? Is there one thing you can identify as something that could help you thrive right now? At this very moment? What can help you move towards being the best version of yourself?

CONTINUOUS GROWTH IS THE GOAL

Thriving is an important concept to embrace. This process of personal growth and focus on well-being has several key elements important to think about (see Figure 6.2). These elements contribute to personal growth. Yes! We know this list has a lot of concepts on it! And yes, it would be difficult to work on all these things every moment of every day. However, if we know what these elements are that can support in thriving as a culturally informed leader than we can intentionally improve.

Central to thriving and focusing on continuous growth is having a purpose in life and a sense of meaning (Seligman, 2011). This provides motivation, direction, and fulfillment toward a better version of yourself

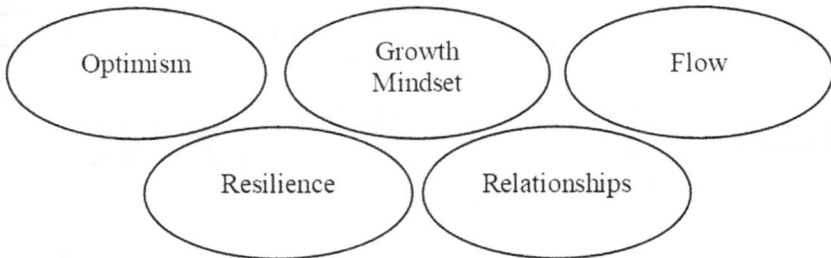

Figure 6.2 Elements of thriving.

and overall well-being. Other aspects such as optimism, growth mindset, engagement and flow, relationships, and resilience are also important to thriving. Let's explore these concepts more in depth.

Optimism is an important part of thriving. Optimism is the tendency to expect positive outcomes. Those who think positively tend to have better health, greater achievement, and resilience (Seligman, 2006). It makes sense; optimistic people are more likely to thrive because they approach life with hope and positivity. Although being optimist is not always easy, a sense of hope is important to strive for, especially when leading others. Some are more naturally positive than others, but optimism is something we can practice and intentionally reflect on, especially in more difficult times.

Another critical aspect of thriving is having a **growth mindset**. Stanford Professor of Psychology, Carol Dweck (2006) introduced the concept of growth mindset. A growth mindset focuses on putting energy toward learning. Just as we discussed in Chapter 3, centering yourself as a learner is an important aspect of being a culturally informed leader. When you put energy toward leadership learning specifically, you can develop your capacity to lead and follow through various experiences. This includes learning different strategies and how to navigate complicated situations while incorporating feedback of others (Guthrie et al., 2021). This growth mindset is essential when situated in various cultural contexts. Another great thing about a growth mindset is that it fosters a love of learning, which leads to resilience (which we will talk about).

Thriving is also connected with engaging deeply in activities. As we discussed in Chapter 4, engaging in the world around us is important to not only being a culturally informed leader, but contributes to thriving as a person. Czikszentmihalyi (2008) talked about being in a state of **flow** when engaging in activities that lead to satisfaction. Flow is when you are fully immersed in an activity, and you experience not only deep concentration but are enjoying it. Often in a state of flow, people lose track of time and have a sense of mastery in whatever they are doing. This could be playing a sport, doing something artistic like drawing a picture, or leading a group in an activity, like a community service project. Oftentimes creativity is a part of a flow state because it allows people to express themselves, solve problems, or adapt to new situations, all which are vital for thriving.

> **STOP** Have you ever been learning, engaging, or connecting with a different culture and lost track of time? What were you doing? What was it about the activity that allowed you to fully immerse in it? How did you feel after you completed the activity?

Having **relationships** and strong, supportive, social connections are fundamental to thriving and our overall well-being. Having deep relationships with others not only provide emotional support and a sense of belonging, but also opportunities for personal development. When you have close connections with others, reflection, learning, and growth become positive experiences. I am sure you have been hearing about the benefits of having strong relationships since you were a child. Connections with others are the core of well-being and becoming the best version of ourselves. From a leadership learning framework, relationships are at the heart of influencing others in the leadership process, whether that is from a leader or follower role. Building connections with others in various cultural contexts help your journey of being a culturally informed leader through learning, engaging, and connecting with others.

Resilience is also key to thriving. Resilience is the capacity to navigate and adapt to stressors and adversity all while maintaining a state of well-being. Coping with stress, adversity, and change are all hallmark to being resilient (Richardson, 2002). Individuals who are resilient thrive because they can effectively manage challenges and change, and are also more self-aware, reflective in nature, and believe they can make decisions that guide their own life. It makes sense that resilience, this action of being able to navigate and adapt contributes to thriving and progression forward. However, to fully thrive we also need to think about the need for a balance of being challenged and having support. If we are challenged too much, we can shut down. If we are supported and praised too much, we don't work to be better, we can become stagnant. So, to focus on thriving, it must include resilience, as well as support and challenge.

Optimism, growth mindset, engagement and flow, relationships, and resilience are all interrelated factors and contribute to a holistic sense of thriving. This, as well as other aspects, allow for individuals to move beyond just surviving and enter a state of continuous improvement, which is important to strive for as a culturally informed leader. Intentional continuous growth, as we have discussed in this entire book, is central to your leadership learning journey and we know you are here for it.

PUTTING THE PUZZLE TOGETHER: LEARNING, ENGAGING, AND CONNECTING

Throughout this book, we have discussed several aspects of being a culturally informed leader. Just as pieces of a puzzle, being able to learn, engage, and connect in various cultural contexts is critical to working for a better world. As you can see in Figure 6.3, the puzzle pieces are fitting back together. In this book, we introduced different theories and ways you can learn, engage, and connect. We provided opportunities to explore how you can practice being a culturally informed leader. We encouraged you to reflect on how you are currently learning, engaging, and connecting, as well as how you can do this in the future as a culturally informed leader. Please

Figure 6.3 Culturally informed puzzle.

hear us when we say how important it is to keep learning, engaging, and connecting. Every single day. Let us say this again, keep learning, engaging, and connecting every single day to be culturally informed. If you look around, you will find these opportunities easily, especially when engaging in various cultural contexts. As we know, our personal experiences influence our understanding and practice of leadership, especially in various cultural contexts. However, the goal should always be focused on being the best leader and follower we can be-no matter what the context or situation is. This means you should strive to not only thrive, but to be the best version of yourself. The best version of YOU. Not your friend, sibling, or anyone else, but YOU. You have so much to offer this world, and we need you.

We are all on a leadership learning journey together. Ever. Single. One. Of. Us. Sure, there are people who have more and less experiences than you do. The important part of this journey is that you are not alone, especially when it comes to being culturally informed. We learn culturally informed leadership not only for the betterment of ourselves, but for others. We strive to make the communities we live in better. We strive for positive change. When we thrive, those around us thrive also. If we strive to learn something each day, engage with others in meaningful ways, and make connections in this complex world, we will continue to develop as a culturally informed leader. This book is not about arriving at a destination but continuing this leadership learning journey together, which is global in nature. As Figure 6.3 shows, we can continue to put the puzzle pieces together to build more culturally informed leaders. We look forward to being with you on this journey as we work to collectively make this world better. You matter in this world.

REFLECT ON YOUR OWN

- How often do you seek out learning opportunities to deepen your understanding of various cultures? What about regarding your own leadership learning?
- Of the aspects discussed in thriving as a culturally informed leader, what do you find most challenging? How can you develop this area further?
- Thriving is about being on the journey of growth to being the best version of yourself. When you think about the best version of yourself as a culturally informed leader, what is the first thing that comes to mind?

REFLECT WITH A FRIEND

- Thriving is about having a sense of meaning. When thinking about learning, engaging, and connecting in various cultural contexts, what meaning can you make from your motivation to do this? In other words, what motivates you to being a culturally informed leader?
- How do you model culturally informed behavior to inspire and influence others around you?
- What are some ideas to measure your growth as a culturally informed leader over time?

LEVELING UP!

Activity 1: Thriving Tree

As we have discussed in this chapter, being a culturally informed leader means focusing on ways to thrive. There are several aspects of thriving including, but not limited to optimism, growth mindset, engagement and flow, relationships, and resilience. This activity will help you intentionally think about ways to contribute to your overall sense of thriving. This tree represents your life and how if you tend to the foundation of your life, the roots and where you are currently at, the trunk, the branches and leaves will be allowed to grow and thrive. Think about where you are at currently in your leadership learning journey.

- At the roots of the tree, your foundation, think about what supports you and is foundational to your being. This can be concepts, people, places or experiences. For example, family support, education, faith, resilience, or positivity.
- At the trunk of the tree, write words or phrases of your current state of leadership learning. Are you feeling strong? Stable? Growing? Challenged? Reflect honestly on your current state of leadership learning.
- On the branches, identify areas that help you thrive. This might relate to the areas we discussed in this chapter such as optimism,

growth mindset, engagement and flow, relationships, and resilience. However, it could also be other areas like creativity, physical health, learning, community involvement, or anything else that helps you to thrive.

- Finally, draw leaves on the branches and write specific habits, actions, or people that support the areas of thriving you chose. An example may be meditation or journal writing for optimism.

Once you have completed your tree, reflect on one or two actions you can take in the next few weeks to strengthen a specific area of your leadership learning journey and move you toward thriving as a culturally informed leader.

Activity 2: Concept Mapping

You did it! You reached the end of this book. Hopefully you find yourself thinking about the different concepts you have learned. But you may be thinking about how all of this connects with me as a culturally informed leader. To explore this in more depth, let's use a concept map. Concept maps allow us to visually explore connections of concepts. In the visual below, you will see that this starts with you. In the six circles around the box, write key terms, phrases, theories, models, or concepts you learned in this book. Take it a step further and write one to two more detailed concepts, terms, or phrases about those elements in shapes you created. Draw lines between the box and the circles, and the shapes you added. Do you see your concept map start to grow? Add layers as you see how these concepts connect. This activity doubles as a simple, but effective synthesis tool to remember all the things you learned in this book.

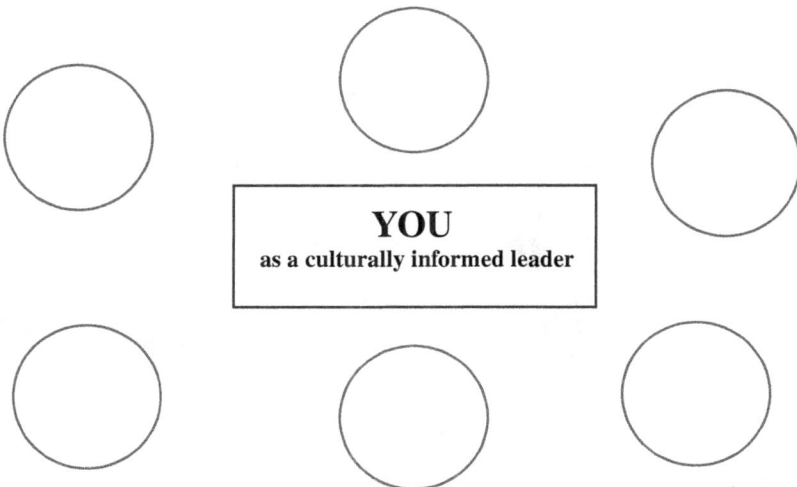

YOU
as a culturally informed leader

ABOUT THE AUTHORS

Dr. Kathy L. Guthrie grew up on a farm in Central Illinois, which was very influential in her identity as a leader. Kathy remembers learning about leadership while participating in her local 4-H club and various activities in high school like student council, class officer, show choir, captain of cheerleading squad, and running track. While an undergraduate student, she served as an orientation leader, on the campus programming board, as a peer mentor for first year students, and worked in admissions. All these opportunities provided Kathy with experience in engaging in the leadership process. As a Professor of Higher Education at Florida State University, Kathy has taught leadership all over the world. Her research focuses on learning leadership and the outcomes and environment of leadership education. Prior to becoming a faculty member, Kathy served as a student affairs administrator for 10 years in various areas including campus activities, commuter services, community engagement, and leadership development. She has worked in higher education administrative and faculty roles for over 20 years and loves every minute of her chosen career path. Kathy enjoys spending time with her daughter, husband, and dog where collectively all four of them are affectionately known as Team Guthrie.

Dr. Darren E. Pierre is an educator, speaker, and author. From the blissful city of Mebane, North Carolina, Darren is anchored by two quotes: "The ache for home lives in all of us, the safe place where we can come as we are and not be questioned." This quote by Dr. Maya Angelou fortifies Darren's work, scholarship and purpose as an educator within higher education and beyond. Currently, Dr. Pierre serves as a Senior Lecturer in the A. James Clark School of Engineering and Affiliate Faculty in the College of Education at University of Maryland-College Park. Darren has worked in higher education for over 20 years, with past leadership and involvement in associations/organizations including: The Association of Fraternity and Sorority Advisors (AFA), NASPA, ACPA, LeaderShape and the International Leadership Association. Now and beyond, the second quote guiding Darren's service is the African proverb, "when deeds speak, words are nothing."

REFERENCES

Abes, E. S., Jones, S. R., & McEwen, M. K. (2007). Reconceptualizing the model of multiple dimensions of identity: The role of meaning-making capacity in the construction of multiple identities. *Journal of College Student Development, 48*(1), 1–22. https://doi.org/10.1353/csd.2007.0000

Adichie, C. N. (2009, July). The danger of a single story [video]. *Ted Global Conference.* https://www.ted.com/talks/chimamanda_ngozi_adichie_the_danger_of_a_single_story?subtitle=en

Beatty, C. C., & Guthrie, K. L. (2021). *Operationalizing culturally relevant leadership learning*. Information Age Publishing.

Bertrand Jones, T., Guthrie, K. L., & Osteen, L. (2016). Critical domains of culturally relevant leadership learning: A call to transform leadership programs. *New Directions for Student Leadership, 152*, 9–21. https://doi.org/10.1002/yd.20205

Billsberry, J. (2009). The social construction of leadership education. *Journal of Leadership Education, 8*(2), 1–9. https://doi.org/10.12806/v8/i2/ab1

Czikszentmihalyi, M. (2008). *Flow: The psychology of optimal experience*. HarperCollins Publishers.

Del Vitto, C. (2008). Cross-cultural "soft skills" and the global engineer: Corporate best practices and trainer methodologies. *Online Journal for Global Engineering Education, 3*(1). https://digitalcommons.uri.edu/ojgee/vol3/iss1/1?utm_source=digitalcommons.uri.edu%2Fojgee%2Fvol3%2Fiss1%2F1&utm_medium=PDF&utm_campaign=PDFCoverPages

Devies, B. (2022). Making the world your classroom: Observation as a pedagogical tool for leadership learning. In K. L. Guthrie & K. L. Priest (Eds.), *Navigating complexities in leadership: Moving toward critical hope* (pp. 99–108). Information Age Publishing.

Dugan, J. P., & Associates. (2011). Research on college student leadership. In S. R. Komives, J. P. Dugan, J. E. Owen, C. Slack, & W. Wagner (Eds.), *The handbook for student leadership development* (2nd ed., pp. 59–85). Jossey-Bass.

Dugan, J. P. (2017). *Leadership theory: Cultivating critical perspectives.* Jossey-Bass.

Dweck, C. (2006). *Mindset: The new psychology of success*. Random House.

Ferraro, G. (2009). *Cultural dimensions of global business* (6th ed.). Prentice Hall.

Ferraro, G., & Briody, E. (2017). *The cultural dimensions of global business* (8th ed.). Routledge.

Fiske, S. T., & Taylor, S. E. (1991). *Social cognition* (2nd ed.). McGraw-Hill.

Gundling, E., & Williams, C. (2021). *Inclusive leadership, global impact* (2nd ed.). Aperian Global.

Guthrie, K. L., Beatty, C. C., & Wiborg, E. (2021). *Engaging in the leadership process: Identity, capacity, and efficacy for college students.* Information Age Publishing.

Guthrie, K. L., & Devies, B. (2024). *Foundations of leadership: Principles, practice, and progress.* Information Age Publishing.

Guthrie, K. L., & Jenkins, D. M. (2018). *The role of leadership educators: Transforming learning.* Information Age Publishing.

Guthrie, K. L., & Jenkins, D. M. (2024). Shifting from education to learning: Leadership learning framework. *New Directions for Student Leadership, 183,* 13–22. https://doi.org/10.1002/yd.20619

Harper, D. (2024). Context. *Online Etymology Dictionary.* https://www.etymonline.com/word/context. Accessed June 18, 2024.

Higher Education Research Institute (HERI). (1996). *A social change model of leadership development (Version III).* University of California, Los Angeles Higher Education Research Institute.

Jones, S. R., & Abes, E. S. (2013). *Identity development of college students: Advancing frameworks for multiple dimensions of identity.* John Wiley & Sons.

Korac-Kakabadse, N., Kouzmin, A., Korac-Kakabadse, , A., & Savery, L. (2001). Lowand high-context communication patterns: Towards mapping cross-cultural encounters. *Cross Cultural Management: An International Journal, 8*(2), 3–24. https://doi.org/10.1108/13527600110797218

Lane, H. W., & Maznevski, M. L. (2014). *International management behavior: Global and sustainable leadership* (7th ed.). Wiley.

Lord, R. G., & Maher, K. J. (1991). *Leadership and information processing: Linking perceptions and performance.* Routledge.

Mendenhall, M. E., Osland, J., Bird, A., Oddou, G. R., Maznevski, M. L., Stevens, M., & Stahl, G. K. (2012). *Global leadership: Research, practice, and development* (2nd ed.). Routledge.

Mendenhall, M. E., Osland, J., Bird, A., Oddou, G. R., Stevens, M., Maznevski, M. L., & Stahl, G. K. (2018). *Global leadership: Research, practice, and development* (3rd ed.). Routledge.

Moreno-Aponte, M., & Koulouris, K. (2017). Cross-cultural dimensions of personal stories in communicating authentic leadership. In J. L. Chin, J. E. Trimble, & J. E. Garcia, (Eds.), *Global and culturally diverse leaders and leadership: New dimensions and challenges for business, education and society (2018)* (pp. 41-62). Emerald Publishing.

Ng, K. Y., Dyne, L. V., & Ang, S. (2009). Developing global leaders: The role of international experience and cultural intelligence. *Advances in Global Leadership, 5,* 225–250.

Niesen, C. C. (2010). Navigating reentry shock: The use of communication as a facilitative tool. https://digitalrepository.unm.edu/cj_etds/60

Nirenberg, J. (2002). *Global leadership.* Capstone Publishing.

Noon, M. (2018). Pointless diversity training: Unconscious bias, new racism and agency. *Work, Employment & Society, 32*(1), 198–209. https://doi.org/10.1177/0950017017719841

Northouse, P. G. (2022). *Leadership: Theory and practice* (9th ed.). SAGE.

Oberg, K. (1960). Cultural shock: Adjustment to new cultural environments. *Missiology: An International Review, 7*(4), 177–182. https://doi.org/10.1177/009182966000700405

Osland, J. (2012). An overview of global literature. In M. E. Mendenhall, J. Osland, B. Oddou, G. R. Maznevski, M. Stevens, G. K. Stahl.(Eds.), *Global leadership 2e: Research, practice, and development (2012)*. Routledge.

Patton, L. D., Renn, K. A., Guido, F. M., & Quaye, S. J. (2016). *Student development in college : Theory, research, and practice* (3rd ed.). Jossey-Bass.

Pontes, M., & Weng, J. (2024). Leadership development research & scholarship. *New Directions for Student Leadership, 183*, 43–49. https://doi.org/10.1002/yd.20622

Richardson, G. E. (2002). The metatheory of resilience and resiliency. *Journal of Clinical Psychology, 58*, 307–321. https://doi.org/10.1002/jclp.10020

Risku, K., & Holder, C. (2024). Understanding engagement as a catalyst for leadership learning. *New Directions for Student Leadership, 183*, 103–110. https://doi.org/10.1002/yd.20631

Rocco, M. L., & Rupert Davis, K. (2024). Expanding the boundaries of leadership development: Propositions for leadership educators. *New Directions for Student Leadership, 183*, 51–58. https://doi.org/10.1002/yd.20623

Seligman, M. E. (2006). *Learned optimism: How to change your mind and your life.* Vintage.

Seligman, M. E. (2011). *Flourish: A visionary new understanding of happiness and well-being.* Simon and Schuster.

Shankman, M. L., Allen, S. J., & Haber-Curran, P. (2015). *Emotionally intelligent leadership: A guide for students* (2nd ed.). Jossey-Bass.

Sowcik, M. (2012). Legitimacy, maturity, and accountability of leadership studies programs: A movement towards "good" practices. *Journal of Leadership Studies, 6*(3), 47–48. https://doi.org/10.1002/jls.21255

Stanford, S. (2022). Diversity, bias, and impacting change: Systems of thought and behaviors within bias and inequity. In *SAGE skills: Student success*. SAGE. https://doi.org/10.4135/9781071900536

Thomas, D. C., & Inkson, K. (2017). *Cultural intelligence: Surviving and thriving in the global village* Ser. Business professional collection (3rd ed.). Berrett-Koehler Publishers.

Ting-Toomey, S., & Chung, L. C. (2012). *Understanding intercultural communication* (2nd ed.). Oxford University Press.

Turnbull, H. (2016). *The illusion of inclusion: Global inclusion, unconscious bias, and the bottom line.* Business Expert Press.

United Nations Department of Economic and Social Affairs, Population Division (2022). *World population prospects 2022: Summary of results. UN DESA/POP/2022/TR/NO. 3.*